Is Marijuana Harmful?

Bradley Steffens

San Diego, CA

About the Author

Bradley Steffens is a poet, playwright, novelist, and author of thirty nonfiction books for children and young adults. He is a two-time recipient of the San Diego Book Award for Best Young Adult and Children's Nonfiction: His *Giants* won the 2005 award, and his *J.K. Rowling* claimed the 2007 prize. Steffens also received the Theodor S. Geisel Award for best book by a San Diego County author in 2007.

© 2017 ReferencePoint Press, Inc.
Printed in the United States

For more information, contact:
ReferencePoint Press, Inc.
PO Box 27779
San Diego, CA 92198
www.ReferencePointPress.com

LIBRARY OF CONGRESS CATALOGING-IN-PUBLICATION DATA

Names: Steffens, Bradley, 1955-
Title: Is marijuana harmful? / by Bradley Steffens.
Description: San Diego, CA : ReferencePoint Press, Inc., 2017. | Series:
    Issues in society | Includes bibliographical references and index.
Identifiers: LCCN 2016013723 (print) | LCCN 2016017169 (ebook) | ISBN
    9781682820971 (hardback) | ISBN 9781682821008 (eBook)
Subjects: LCSH: Marijuana abuse--United States--Juvenile literature. |
    Marijuana--Therapeutic use--United States--Juvenile literature. |
    Marijuana--Law and legislation--United States--Juvenile literature.
Classification: LCC HV5822.M3 P53 2017 (print) | LCC HV5822.M3 (ebook) | DDC
    362.29/5--dc23
LC record available at https://lccn.loc.gov/2016013723

CONTENTS

The World's Illicit Drug of Choice

Marijuana, also known as cannabis, is the most widely used illicit drug in the world. According to the United Nations (UN), more than 246 million people use the drug each year. Some use marijuana as a type of medicine to relieve pain or to treat other symptoms of illness. Others, such as the Rastafari, use it in religious ceremonies as an aid to meditation. But the vast majority of marijuana users consume the drug for recreational purposes. Many people see nothing wrong with using marijuana for enjoyment and have campaigned for years to have the drug legalized. Others, however, believe marijuana use has personal and social costs that outweigh its recreational value.

Increasing Usage

The United States has more marijuana users than any nation in the world. According to the UN, about 44 million Americans used marijuana at least once in the past year. While the percentage of people using marijuana globally has stabilized at about 5 percent, the percentage of Americans who use the drug continues to grow and now stands at about 14 percent.

The increase in marijuana use in the United States is due in part to the changing legal status of the drug. Forty-one states allow the use of some form of marijuana for medical purposes. Four states and the District of Columbia have legalized marijuana for recreational purposes. Colorado was the first state to legalize the commercial sale of marijuana. By 2016, more than six hundred marijuana dispensaries were selling the drug in the Rocky Mountain state. According to the Colorado Department of Revenue, there now are more marijuana dispensaries operating in Colorado than McDonald's and Starbucks restaurants combined.

Many experts are concerned about the effect the legalization of marijuana will have on the people who use the drug and on society as a whole. The UN's International Narcotics Control Board (INCB), which coordinates global efforts to counter drug trafficking, has expressed concern that the United States and other nations are not living up to the 1961 Single Convention on Narcotic Drugs, a protocol created by the United Nations that limits uses of marijuana. "The Board is concerned that a number of States that are parties to the 1961 Convention are considering legislative proposals intended to regulate the use of cannabis for purposes other than medical and scientific ones," wrote the INCB. "The Board therefore urges all Governments and the international community to carefully consider the negative impact of such developments. In the Board's opinion, the likely increase in the abuse of cannabis will lead to an increase in related public health costs."[1]

> "The likely increase in the abuse of cannabis will lead to an increase in related public health costs."[1]
>
> —International Narcotics Control Board (INCB), an office within the United Nations that coordinates global efforts to stop illegal drug trafficking

Documented Dangers

A great deal of scientific evidence stands behind the INCB's concerns. Studies have shown that marijuana use impairs memory and cognitive performance, alters brain structure, and is linked to increased risks of psychosis and suicide. A study conducted at Duke University followed 1,037 subjects from birth through age thirty-eight. The researchers gave the subjects psychological tests at age thirteen, before any of them had used marijuana, and again at age thirty-eight, when some had used the drug. The researchers compared the test scores only of subjects with the same amounts of education, to rule out any effects that years of education might have on IQ. They found that "persistent cannabis use was associated with neuropsychological decline broadly across domains of functioning, even after controlling for years of education."[2]

The Duke University study noted the impairment was greater for those who started using marijuana in adolescence. Researchers at Harvard University and Northwestern University may have discovered a clue about why that might be. A 2014 comparison of brain scans among young adults found differences between those who used marijuana and those who did not. The differences showed up in the structure of an area of the brain known

An eye-catching medical marijuana dispensary in Venice Beach, California, stands out among other boardwalk businesses. California is one of forty-one states that allow the use of some form of marijuana for medical purposes.

as the nucleus accumbens. This part of the brain "is at the core of motivation, the core of pleasure and pain, and every decision that you make,"[3] said Dr. Hans Breiter, coauthor of the study. The researchers found that the more marijuana a user consumed, the greater the changes in brain structure.

Some studies suggest changes in brain structure do not occur among people who start using marijuana as adults. Other studies show the use of marijuana affects memory, thinking, and behavior in adults; however, the symptoms are not permanent if a person stops using the drug. These studies suggest marijuana is safe as long as it is consumed during adulthood, not adolescence, marijuana advocates say. They point out it is still against the law for adolescents to use marijuana in states where recreational use has been legalized.

Declining Perceptions of Risk

That might be true, critics of legalization point out, but alcohol consumption also is prohibited under age twenty-one, yet underage drinking is widespread. Critics say the same thing will happen if marijuana use is legalized, in part because legalization sends a message that marijuana is safe. "Teens' perceptions of the risks of marijuana use have steadily declined over the past decade, possibly related to increasing public debate about legalizing or loosening restrictions on marijuana for medicinal and recreational use,"[4] stated the US Department of Health and Human Services.

Legalization drives down the cost of marijuana, making it more affordable to young people. Research shows marijuana consumption increases as the drug's price decreases. "It is estimated that for each 10 per cent drop in price, there will be an approximately 3 per cent increase in the total number of users and a 3–5 per cent increase in youth initiation,"[5] warns the United Nations Office on Drugs and Crime (UNODC).

> "Teens' perceptions of the risks of marijuana use have steadily declined over the past decade."[4]
>
> —US Department of Health and Human Services, a cabinet-level department of the federal government

Buoyed by their success in Colorado and other states, marijuana advocates are pushing to legalize the drug across the United States. Businesses, too, are eager to cash in on the market opportunities presented by legalization in populous states such as New York and California. As public officials and voters consider legalizing marijuana, they must weigh both the positive effects that legalizing the drug might have on the states' economies and tax revenues and the negative effects legalization might have on public safety and personal health.

CHAPTER 1

What Are the Facts?

Marijuana is a Spanish word for the dried leaves, stems, and flowers of *Cannabis sativa*, the hemp plant. Like all plants, the hemp plant is made up of many different chemical compounds. The chemical makeup of a plant determines what use, if any, it has for human beings. Some plants, such as lettuce and celery, are nutritious. Others, such as nightshade, are poisonous. Still others, such as basil and ginger, have medicinal properties. The hemp plant contains more than seven hundred different chemical compounds. One of these compounds is known as delta-9-tetrahydrocannabinol, or THC. When ingested, THC affects a person's brain. For this reason, marijuana is considered a psychoactive, or mind-altering, drug. Other compounds in marijuana have been shown to have medicinal qualities. These compounds can alleviate pain, reduce nausea, and help control seizures.

How THC Works

THC belongs to a class of chemical compounds known as cannabinoids. These compounds are made up of various molecules arranged in similar ways. The hemp plant contains at least 113 different cannabinoids, known as phytocannabinoids. The human body also produces cannabinoids as part of its normal functioning. These naturally occurring cannabinoids are known as endogenous cannabinoids, or endocannabinoids.

Endocannabinoids play an important role in the functioning of the human nervous system. They allow nerve cells, known as neurons, to transmit chemical messages to one another. As a result, endocannabinoids are known as neurotransmitters. They work by attaching themselves to molecules on neurons called cannabinoid receptors and then stimulating the neuron.

One cannabinoid produced by the body is known as anandamide. This compound is nearly identical in its chemical makeup and structure to marijuana's THC. As a result, when THC is introduced into the human body, it behaves exactly like anandamide. It fits into cannabinoid receptors like a key in a lock. Once in place, THC sends a chemical signal to the neuron, just as anandamide would. However, since THC was not produced as part of the body's neural communication network, the message it sends is not part of the body's normal functioning. In this sense, THC disrupts the nervous system's communications.

While the nervous system extends throughout the entire body, the greatest concentration of neurotransmitters is in the brain. The chemical messages sent between the brain's neurons govern thinking, mood, memory, concentration, movement, coordination, the perception of time, and many other functions. When

Marijuana comes from the dried leaves, stems, and flowers of the plant known as Cannabis sativa *(pictured). The psychoactive, or mind-altering, effects of marijuana result from the naturally occurring chemical compound THC.*

Introducing THC Into the Body

To find its way to the cannabinoid receptors in the brain, THC must enter the bloodstream. This can be accomplished in several ways. A user can smoke marijuana in the form of a small, hand-rolled cigarette, called a joint, or in a cigar in which most or all of the tobacco has been removed, known as a blunt. Many users smoke marijuana in a straight glass pipe known as a glass. Others use a water pipe, sometimes called a bong. Some users, especially those using marijuana for medicinal purposes, mix the shredded leaves into food, such as cookies or brownies, or use the dried plant to make a tea.

Since most of the hemp plant's THC is found in its resin, some marijuana processors extract the resin and use it to make substances with high concentrations of THC, including an oil known as hash oil, a waxy substance known as budder, and a hard material known as shatter. The user heats these concentrated forms of marijuana and then inhales the vapor or smoke. Marijuana's active ingredient is so concentrated in these forms that a dose as small as the head of a pin is enough to produce a psychoactive effect.

When a marijuana user inhales smoke from the leaves or the resin, the active ingredients pass through the lungs and directly into the bloodstream. Since most marijuana users take the drug for pleasure or recreation, they usually smoke the drug so they can experience its psychoactive effects as quickly as possible.

THC attaches to cannabinoid receptors in the brain, it can affect many of these functions.

When THC becomes attached to neurons in certain regions of the brain, it can stimulate the neurons to release a chemical known as dopamine. This chemical produces a pleasurable sensation. Dopamine normally is released during enjoyable activities such as eating, drinking, and having sex. The chemical acts as a kind of "reward system" for doing things that ensure the body's health, survival, and procreation. By stimulating the release of dopamine, THC can give the user of marijuana a pleasant feeling, or "high."

When THC attaches to neurons in other parts of the brain, it can stimulate the release of chemicals that create other sensations or emotions, including fear, distrust, anxiety, and panic. In extreme cases, especially when a person consumes a large amount of THC, the chemical can trigger psychosis, which can include hallucinations, delusions, or confusion about one's identity.

Because of marijuana's intoxicating nature, many governments around the world have outlawed its cultivation, sale, possession, and use. Other governments prohibit growing, distributing, and selling marijuana, although not its use or its possession in small amounts. Because of these laws, marijuana is classified by governments and by organizations such as the United Nations as an illicit, or illegal, drug.

Global Marijuana Use

Despite its status as an illicit drug, hundreds of millions of people use marijuana worldwide. According to the United Nations Office on Drugs and Crime (UNODC), between 128 million and 232 million people aged fifteen to sixty-four used marijuana at least once in the past year. This corresponds to between 2.7 percent and 4.9 percent of the world population, making marijuana the world's most widely consumed illicit drug and the third most used recreational drug, after alcohol and tobacco. If all the people who used marijuana in the past year formed a nation, it would be the fifth most populous country in the world, larger than Brazil, Pakistan, Nigeria, Bangladesh, Russia, and 186 other countries. Approximately six times as many people use marijuana as the next most widely used group of illicit drugs—opiates. In addition, the number of marijuana users continues to grow worldwide, while the use of opiates has remained steady and the use of cocaine and amphetamines has declined.

Marijuana is used in nearly every nation in the world, although the percentages of users vary widely from country to country. For example, 29.5 percent of the people in Papua New Guinea report using marijuana at least once a year, compared to just 0.1 percent in Japan, according to the UNODC. Differences in a country's culture, religion, and laws have more of an effect on usage than the relative wealth of its population or the cost of the drug. For example, Qatar has the world's highest per capita income, but because of its strict laws and conservative religious culture, it ranks 158th in the world for marijuana usage. Singapore, another wealthy nation, hands down the death penalty for possession of more than half an ounce of marijuana. Not surprisingly, it reports the world's lowest marijuana usage rate, with just 0.004 percent of the population having used the drug in the last year.

According to the UNODC, the United States ranks twelfth in the world for marijuana use by a percentage of the population, with 13.7 percent of Americans having consumed the drug at least once in the last year. Because the United States is the most populous of the leading marijuana-consuming countries, it ranks first for the total number of marijuana users, with 43.8 million, including 22 million who used the drug in the past month. India ranks second in the world for the total number of marijuana users with 38.4 million, even though just 3.2 percent of the country's 1.2 billion people consumed marijuana in the last year. Canada ranks just behind the United States in the percentage of the population using marijuana at 12.6 percent. Because of its smaller population, Canada ranks tenth in the world in total number of marijuana users. The other nations in the top ten for total number of marijuana users are Nigeria, Italy, Pakistan, Ghana, France, Egypt, and Spain.

Marijuana use cuts across culture, race, and economic status. However, there is a distinct difference in the use of the drug by gender. Worldwide, men are three times more likely than women to use marijuana. According to the UNODC, the difference in marijuana use between the sexes "mainly reflects differences in opportunities to use drugs due to the influence of the social or cultural environment rather than intrinsic gender vulnerability." The illicit nature of marijuana seems to deter women from using the drug. When women can purchase a substance legally, they are more willing to use it. "Women are more likely than men to misuse prescription drugs, particularly prescription opioids and tranquilizers,"[6] states the UNODC.

Marijuana Use by Young Adults

Percentages of marijuana users vary by age as well. Marijuana use peaks during adolescence and declines as people get older. Ac-

Teenagers represent the largest group of marijuana users. It is the drug of choice for this age group in many countries, including the United States, Canada, Australia, and several countries in Europe.

cording to a 2015 report on adolescent drug use by the Institute for Social Research at the University of Michigan, 11.8 percent of eighth graders in the United States reported using marijuana in the past year, a rate approaching the overall national average of 13.7 percent. Among tenth graders, however, the rate was nearly double the national average, with 25.4 percent reporting they had used the drug in the past year. By twelfth grade, the number of young adults who said they had used the drug in the last year stood at 34.9 percent, more than two-and-a-half times the national average. Many of these users had merely experimented with the drug, but 21.3 percent reported they had used the drug in the last month, making them current users. Fully 6 percent of twelfth graders reported using marijuana on a daily or near-daily basis.

Young adults use marijuana far more than any other illicit substance. According to the UN's *World Youth Report*, marijuana accounts for 90 percent of all illicit drug use among teens in the United States and Australia. In Europe, the percentage is even higher, with marijuana accounting for 95 percent of all illicit drug use. In Australia, Canada, France, Ireland, the United Kingdom, and the United States, an average of 25 percent of secondary school students report using marijuana in the past year.

Social scientists have identified many reasons that a higher percentage of adolescents use marijuana than do older adults. Summarizing the findings of several different studies, the *World Youth Report* states:

> Young people use substances for many of the same reasons adults do (to relieve stress or heighten enjoyment); however, there are some reasons for use that arise from needs specifically related to adolescent development. Sources of motivation include the desire to take risks, demonstrate autonomy and independence, develop values distinct from parental and societal authority, signal entry into a peer group, seek novel and exciting experiences, and satisfy curiosity.[7]

Marijuana use declines after adolescence for a number of reasons. Some of the unique drivers of adolescent usage such as satisfying curiosity no longer apply once a person has tried the substance. In addition, the potential negative consequences of using an illegal drug are much more important to adults. Public records, such as drug convictions, are readily available online, and many prospective employers use such information to screen out job applicants. A conviction of possession of marijuana can result in lost job opportunities. In addition many companies require new hires to pass a drug test before starting work, and some even require drug tests during the time of employment. THC-COOH, the chemical produced by the liver when it breaks down THC, remains in the bloodstream for several days after marijuana use, and in some cases it can be detected in

"Young people use substances for many of the same reasons adults do . . . however, there are some reasons for use that arise from needs specifically related to adolescent development [such as] the desire to take risks, demonstrate autonomy and independence, . . . and satisfy curiosity."[7]

—*World Youth Report*, a publication of the United Nations

the system for more than a month. The possibility of not being hired or of losing one's job because of marijuana use is a major deterrent to using the drug among adults.

The Legal Status of Marijuana

The status of marijuana as an illegal drug is changing, and those changes are affecting the number of users as well. US federal law

A Surge in Marijuana Use

In a 2013 Gallup poll, 38 percent of American adults said they had tried marijuana at some point in their lives. This was only 4 percent more than had reported trying the drug in 1999 and just 5 percent more than in 1985. "Americans' support for legalizing marijuana has grown markedly in the past two decades," wrote Lydia Saad, an analyst with Gallup. "While this might leave the impression that increasing numbers of Americans are using marijuana recreationally, Gallup finds no such surge in Americans' self-reported experience with the drug."

Just two years later, the whole picture had changed. "As Oregon becomes the fourth state to make recreational marijuana use legal, 44% of Americans say they have tried marijuana," wrote Justin McCarthy, an analyst with Gallup. "This is the highest percentage Gallup has found since it began asking the question in 1969." The six-point rise represented an increase of 16 percent from 2013 to 2015. Even more striking, the percentage of adults who said they currently used marijuana rose from 7 percent in 2013 to 11 percent in 2015—a 57 percent surge over two years. "The stigma associated with smoking marijuana appears to be loosening, and Americans may be less shy about revealing their experiences or habits than they have been in the past," wrote McCarthy. "For whatever reason, more Americans than ever before admit that they have smoked marijuana in the past, and there has been an increase in the modest percentage who say they currently smoke it."

Lydia Saad, "In U.S., 38% Have Tried Marijuana, Little Changed Since '80s," Gallup, August 2, 2013. www.gallup.com.

Justin McCarthy, "More than Four in 10 Americans Say They Have Tried Marijuana," Gallup, July 22, 2015. www.gallup.com.

prohibits the cultivation, sale, possession, and use of marijuana. Despite attempts to change marijuana's legal status at the federal level, it remains on Schedule I of the Controlled Substances Act, a category reserved for drugs that the FDA says have "no currently accepted medical use" and "a high potential for abuse."[8]

Eight states and two US territories—Arkansas, Idaho, Indiana, Kansas, North and South Dakota, Pennsylvania, West Virginia, American Samoa, and Northern Mariana Islands—prohibit the sale, possession, and use of any form of marijuana. Seventeen states—Alabama, Florida, Georgia, Iowa, Kentucky, Louisiana, Mississippi, Missouri, North and South Carolina, Oklahoma, Tennessee, Texas, Utah, Virginia, Wisconsin, and Wyoming—prohibit the type of marijuana that produces psychoactive effects. These seventeen states, however, have legalized the use of marijuana with little or no THC for medical purposes. Nine states and two US territories—Arizona, Hawaii, Illinois, Michigan, Montana, New Hampshire, New Jersey, New Mexico, Ohio, Guam, and Puerto Rico—allow psychoactive marijuana, but only for medical use. Eleven states—California, Connecticut, Delaware, Maine, Maryland, Massachusetts, Minnesota, Nevada, New York, Rhode Island, and Vermont—allow psychoactive marijuana for medical use and also have decriminalized possession of small amounts of the drug. In these eleven states, possession can lead to a civil fine but not a criminal conviction. One state and one US territory—Nebraska and the US Virgin Islands—have decriminalized marijuana possession without legalizing its use for medical treatment. Four states—Alaska, Colorado, Oregon, and Washington—and the District of Columbia have legalized marijuana for both medical and recreational use.

Colorado was the first state to legalize the use of marijuana for recreational purposes. "It's heartening to see that tens of thousands of otherwise law-abiding Coloradans have been spared the travesty of getting handcuffed or being charged for small amounts of marijuana," said Art Way, a spokesperson for the Drug Policy Alliance, a group advocating the end of marijuana prohibition. "By focusing on public health rather than criminalization, Colorado is better positioned to address the potential harms of marijuana use, while diminishing many of the worst aspects of the war on drugs."[9]

Colorado and other states that have legalized marijuana are in conflict with federal law, which prohibits recreational marijuana. When conflicts arise between state and federal law, federal law must prevail, according to Article VI, Clause 2 of the US Constitution, known as the Supremacy Clause. However, in the case of marijuana laws, the federal government has not attempted to override the laws of the states. Instead, the US government is allowing the states that have legalized recreational marijuana to function as what are sometimes called "laboratories of democracy." This phrase was used by US Supreme Court justice Louis Brandeis, in his dissent in *New State Ice Co. v. Liebmann*, to

> "It's heartening to see that tens of thousands of otherwise law-abiding Coloradans have been spared the travesty of getting handcuffed or being charged for small amounts of marijuana."[9]
>
> —Art Way, a spokesperson for the Drug Policy Alliance, a group advocating the end of marijuana prohibition

An Iraq War veteran prepares to make the first legal purchase of recreational marijuana in Colorado history on January 1, 2014. Colorado was the first state to legalize the recreational use marijuana.

describe how a "state may, if its citizens choose, serve as a laboratory; and try novel social and economic experiments without risk to the rest of the country."[10]

The legalization of marijuana in the United States has drawn criticism from various international bodies. The INCB wrote,

> The Board is concerned about the implementation of the ballot initiatives that legalized cannabis for non-medical purposes in the United States. The Board underlines that such legislation is not in conformity with the international drug control treaties. The Board urges the Government of the United States to continue to ensure the full implementation of the international drug control treaties on its entire territory.[11]

The INCB worries that America's go-it-alone drug policy will make it harder for the 186 other countries where marijuana is illegal to enforce their laws. The same fear has been expressed by other states within the United States regarding Colorado's experiment with legalization. Nebraska and Oklahoma sued Colorado in the US Supreme Court, claiming that Colorado's policy violates federal law and has increased drug trafficking in their jurisdictions. The Supreme Court declined to hear the case.

Behind the legal wrangling is a concern not only about law enforcement, but also about the impact that increased use of marijuana will have on traffic safety, workplace safety, and various public health concerns. The citizens of Colorado, Oregon, Washington, and Alaska have decided that marijuana is no more harmful than other legal drugs, such as alcohol and tobacco. Now voters and public officials in other states must decide if they agree.

Does Marijuana Adversely Impact Health?

CHAPTER 2

"I missed a lot. A lot of memories aren't there," a woman who used marijuana for forty-four years told Madeleine Winer, a reporter for the *Arizona Republic*. "I raised a son, but I wasn't there mentally at all."[12] The woman's experiences are not usual; scientific studies have found that memory loss is one of the most common effects of chronic marijuana use. When THC attaches to the cannabinoid receptors in the brain, it can prevent the neurons from forming and finding memories. "Cannabinoids impair all stages of memory including encoding, consolidation, and retrieval,"[13] wrote Mohini Ranganathan and Deepak Cyril D'Souza in the scientific review *Psychopharmacology*.

Scientists at Murdoch Childrens Research Institute in Melbourne, Australia, may have found a reason for the loss of memory in marijuana users. The researchers used magnetic resonance imaging (MRI) to scan the brains of fifty-nine people who had used marijuana for an average of fifteen years. The scientists then compared the images to the scans of thirty-three people who had never used marijuana. The researchers found that the brain's white matter—the cells that allow different parts of the brain to communicate with each other—in the brains of marijuana users were reduced by more than 80 percent compared to the white matter of the nonusers. "Our results suggest that long-term cannabis use is hazardous to white matter in the

> "Our results suggest that long-term cannabis use is hazardous to white matter in the developing brain."[14]
>
> —Andrew Zalesky et al., researchers at Murdoch Childrens Research Institute in Melbourne, Australia

developing brain,"[14] stated the researchers. "These differences are linked to memory impairment and concentration," said Marc Seal, a coauthor of the study. "These people can have trouble learning new things and they are going to have trouble remembering things." Unlike gray matter, which stops developing at age eight, white matter continues to develop throughout a person's lifetime. "If you're a teenager and you've got all these natural cannabinoids in your white matter, it's not good to be introducing a lot of external cannabinoids in your system, because it stops the white matter maturing,"[15] said Seal.

Memory impairment is just one of many effects marijuana has been shown to have on users. Marijuana users also have a higher incidence of anxiety disorders, social development problems, learning difficulties, loss of intelligence as measured by intelligence quotient (IQ), psychosis, and suicide. In addition, smoke from the drug can have a harmful effect on the respiratory system.

A Catalyst for Mental Disorders

In addition to impacting white matter, marijuana also affects the brain's gray matter—the seat of human thinking, emotions, and perceptions. By attaching to the brain's cannabinoid receptors, THC can create short-term anxiety, panic, and even psychosis in some users, especially if they are inexperienced with the drug or the dosage of THC is high. Over the years, marijuana growers have been able to produce plants that have a much higher level of THC than did the plants thirty or forty years ago. "We have seen very, very significant increases in emergency room admissions associated with marijuana use that can't be accounted for solely on basis of changes in prevalence rates," said Nora D. Volkow, director of the National Institute on Drug Abuse and coauthor of a study linking high-THC marijuana to paranoia and psychosis. "It can only be explained by the fact that current marijuana has higher potency associated with much greater risk for adverse effects."[16]

Researchers in south London also found a connection between psychosis and the use of high-THC marijuana. The researchers studied 410 patients hospitalized with psychosis and compared their drug history to 370 people of similar ethnic origin, education, and employment status who did not use the drug. "People who used cannabis or skunk [a high-THC form of marijuana] every day were both roughly three times more likely to have a diagnosis of a psychotic disorder than were those who never used cannabis," wrote the researchers. People who used skunk rather than regular marijuana experienced psychosis at an even higher rate. "Compared with those who never used cannabis, individuals who mostly used skunk-like cannabis were . . . more

THC and the brain

Tetrahydrocannabinol (THC), the psychoactive substance found in cannabis, affects the body when marijuana is smoked or otherwise ingested. Located throughout the body, cannabinoid receptors are found in greatest quantity in the brain, particularly in areas that govern coordination, judgment, learning and memory. Some of the areas THC affects:

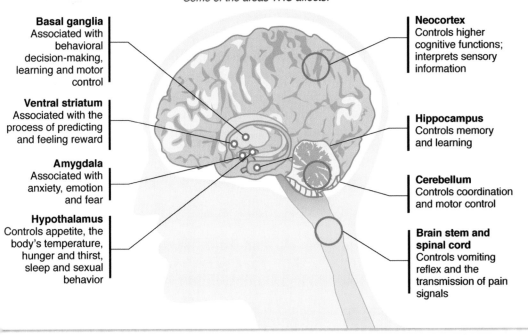

Basal ganglia
Associated with behavioral decision-making, learning and motor control

Ventral striatum
Associated with the process of predicting and feeling reward

Amygdala
Associated with anxiety, emotion and fear

Hypothalamus
Controls appetite, the body's temperature, hunger and thirst, sleep and sexual behavior

Neocortex
Controls higher cognitive functions; interprets sensory information

Hippocampus
Controls memory and learning

Cerebellum
Controls coordination and motor control

Brain stem and spinal cord
Controls vomiting reflex and the transmission of pain signals

than five times as likely [to be diagnosed with a psychotic disorder] if they were daily users."[17]

In 2013 researchers at the National Drug & Alcohol Research Centre, University of New South Wales, Sydney, Australia, found that not only can marijuana cause short-term psychosis, but it also is linked to long-term anxiety disorders. The researchers studied 1,943 subjects over fifteen years, from age fourteen to age twenty-nine. In the study, researchers found that people who used marijuana daily were 2.5 times more likely to have an anxiety disorder than those who did not use the drug. The risk was even higher for those who started using marijuana as adolescents. They were 3.2 times more likely to have an anxiety disorder than those who did not use the drug. "Regular (particularly daily) adolescent cannabis use is associated consistently with anxiety disorder . . . in adolescence and late young adulthood, even among regular users who then cease using the drug,"[18] wrote the researchers.

The use of marijuana in adolescence also has been linked to the loss of IQ. "The most persistent adolescent-onset cannabis users evidenced an average 8-point IQ decline from childhood to adulthood," wrote the authors of a Duke University study that followed subjects from birth to age thirty-eight. "Study members who never used cannabis experienced a slight increase in IQ, whereas those who diagnosed with cannabis dependence . . . experienced IQ declines."[19]

Increased Risks with Variant Genes

Marijuana affects people in different ways, in part because each person's physical makeup is slightly different. Each cell in the human body carries a set of 6.6 billion chemical units known as genes that control how the cells function. Genes vary from person to person (except in the case of identical twins), and these differences show up in many ways—varied hair color, eye color, and other physical traits. Genes also govern the internal organs and chemistry of the body. Studies have found that people carrying certain genes are affected by marijuana in ways that people without those genes are not, making the drug more dangerous for them.

"The most persistent adolescent-onset cannabis users evidenced an average 8-point IQ decline from childhood to adulthood."[19]

—Madeline H. Meier et al., researchers at Duke University Medical Center, Durham, North Carolina

A study led by Marta Di Forti of King's College London found that people who carry a variant of the *AKT1* gene known as *C/C* have increased risk of developing psychosis when using marijuana. The *AKT1* gene governs an enzyme that affects brain signaling involving dopamine, the "reward" chemical that is known to be affected by marijuana but also plays a role in the onset of psychosis. Di Forti and her colleagues found that daily users of marijuana who carried the *C/C* gene variant had a seven times higher risk of developing psychosis than those who used marijuana infrequently or not at all. "Our findings provide strong support for the initial report that genetic variation of AKT1 influences the risk of developing a psychotic disorder in cannabis users,"[20] wrote the researchers.

Another study found an increased risk of psychosis among adults who carry a variant of the gene known as *COMT* and used marijuana in adolescence. "Recent evidence documents that cannabis use by young people is a modest statistical risk factor for psychotic symptoms in adulthood, such as hallucinations and delusions, as well as clinically significant schizophrenia," wrote the researchers. The scientists looked at variants of the *COMT* gene, because this gene governs an enzyme that affects dopamine. People with a variant of the *COMT* gene known as valine[158] create 40 percent less of the enzyme, resulting in higher dopamine levels in the brain when the person uses marijuana. These increased levels of dopamine can trigger the onset of psychosis and schizophrenia. "Carriers of the COMT valine[158] allele were most likely to exhibit psychotic symptoms and to develop schizophreniform disorder if they used cannabis," stated the researchers. "Cannabis use had no such adverse influence on individuals [without the COMT valine[158] allele]."[21]

Some researchers dispute the findings that marijuana can cause long-term psychosis. In 2010 researchers in Rome, Italy, reviewed previous studies about marijuana and psychosis. The researchers found that marijuana intoxication "can lead to acute, transient [short-term] psychotic symptoms," but they were unsure about the drug's long-lasting impact. The researchers found "a consistent association between cannabis use and psychotic symptoms," but added that they could not draw any firm conclusions about whether the drug caused the psychosis. "We conclude that there is insufficient knowledge to determine the level of risk associated with cannabis use in relation to psychotic symptoms,"[22] stated the researchers.

Marijuana and Suicide

Because THC acts directly on the brain and has been shown to cause short-term psychosis in some users and is linked to long-term psychosis in others, scientists wondered if marijuana use might be linked to the recent increase in suicide rates in the United States. The suicide rate in the United States rose by 24 percent from 1999 to 2014, according to the National Center

Marijuana Increases the Risk of Lung Cancer

A large study conducted in Canada found that because marijuana smoke contains many of the same carcinogenic chemicals that are present in tobacco smoke, users are at a greater risk for lung cancer. The researchers drew their conclusions after studying Swedish cause-of-death statistics over a forty-year period for people who were eighteen to twenty years old at the beginning of the period.

5,156 [subjects] reported lifetime use of marijuana and 831 [subjects] indicated lifetime use of more than 50 times, designated as "heavy" use. [We] found that such "heavy" cannabis smoking was significantly associated with more than a twofold risk of developing lung cancer over the 40-year follow-up period, even after statistical adjustment for baseline tobacco use, alcohol use, respiratory conditions, and socioeconomic status. Our primary finding provides initial longitudinal evidence that cannabis use might elevate the risk of lung cancer. In light of the widespread use of marijuana, especially among adolescents and young adults, our study provides important data for informing the risk-benefit calculus of marijuana smoking in medical, public-health, and drug-policy settings.

Russell C. Callaghan et al., "Marijuana Use and Risk of Lung Cancer: A 40-Year Cohort Study," *Cancer Causes and Control*, October 2013. www.ncbi.nlm.nih.gov.

for Health Statistics. Several studies have found a link between marijuana use and suicide. For example, in 2015 a global team of researchers led by Monique Jeanette Delforterie of Vrije Universiteit Amsterdam in the Netherlands studied 9,583 adult twins between the ages of twenty-seven and forty. The researcher team divided suicide attempts into two groups: planned attempts and unplanned attempts. The researchers found that adult marijuana users were 1.9 to 2.5 times more likely to have an unplanned suicide attempt than were nonusers of the drug. "Cannabis involvement is associated, albeit modestly, with suicide ideation [thoughts] and unplanned suicide attempts," wrote the researchers. "Associations persisted even after controlling for other psychiatric disorders and substance involvement."[23]

Two examples of marijuana-related unplanned suicides occurred after Colorado legalized recreational marijuana. Both cases involved edible marijuana, which takes time to produce psychoactive effects. Because of the delayed reaction, inexperienced users sometimes think they have not taken enough of the drug to produce a "high." The results can be tragic. In 2014, a 19-year-old University of Wyoming student named Levy Pongi leapt to his death after consuming a marijuana cookie purchased by a friend. An autopsy showed Pongi had 7.2 nanograms of THC in his blood at the time of his death—about 50 percent higher than the legal limit for driving under the influence of marijuana in Colorado—and no other drugs in his system. Feeling no effects after eating a single piece of the cookie, Pongi consumed the rest of the edible within an hour. Over the next two hours, he showed signs of psychosis, saying irrational things, upending furniture, and tipping over lamps. He then rushed out onto a fourth-floor balcony and jumped to his death. According to investigators, Pongi had never used marijuana before and had no history of alcohol abuse, illicit drug use, or mental illness. The second suicide involved Luke Goodman, a college student who was on a skiing vacation with his family. Family members said Goodman acted extremely irrational after ingesting marijuana candies and then shot himself to death.

As is the case with other disorders, the risk of suicide is highest among marijuana users who started using the drug as teenagers. Researchers in Australia analyzed data involving nearly 3,800

Candy and cookies containing marijuana make for a colorful sales display in an Amsterdam coffee shop. Edible marijuana works slowly in the body, leading some inexperienced users to consume dangerous amounts.

people from Australia and New Zealand in 2014. The researchers compared the behavior of the subjects before age seventeen to various outcomes occurring up to age thirty, including educational attainment, substance use, mental health, and welfare dependence. The study, published in *Lancet Psychiatry*, found that people who started using marijuana before the age of seventeen were seven times more likely to commit suicide than people who never used the drug. "Those who were daily users [of marijuana] before age 17 years had clear reductions in the odds of high-school completion and degree attainment, and substantially increased odds of later cannabis dependence, use of other illicit drugs, and suicide attempt,"[24] wrote the researchers.

Another study found similar results for subjects who began using marijuana before age seventeen. The study led by Michael T. Lynskey of Washington University School of Medicine in St. Louis, Missouri, examined 311 same-sex pairs of twins, one of whom started using marijuana at an early age but the other of whom did not. The advantage of studying identical, or monozygotic, twins is that they share the same genes and usually are raised in the same home. Even twins who are not genetically identical, known as fraternal or dizygotic twins, usually are raised in the same homes. As a result, comparisons between the twins allow researchers to rule out genetic differences and differences in upbringing as factors in the outcomes they find.

The Washington University study found that "those who initiated cannabis use before age 17 years had 3.5 times the odds of reporting a subsequent suicide attempt." The same researchers also looked at 277 same-sex pairs of twins, one of whom had become dependent on marijuana. "Individuals who were cannabis dependent had odds of suicidal ideation [thoughts] and suicide attempt that were 2.5 to 2.9 times higher than those of their non-cannabis-dependent co-twin,"[25] stated the researchers.

> "Those who were daily users [of marijuana] before age 17 years had . . . increased odds of later cannabis dependence, use of other illicit drugs, and suicide attempt."[24]
>
> —Edmund Silins et al., National Drug & Alcohol Research Centre, University of New South Wales, Sydney, Australia

Marijuana and Heart Disease

The brain is not the only organ that researchers have examined for the possible effects of marijuana use. Researchers also have looked at how the drug affects the heart. Within a few minutes of inhaling marijuana smoke, a person's heart rate increases 20 percent to 50 percent. In some cases the heart rate will double, increasing the risk of heart attack. In a study of 3,882 heart attack patients, researchers at Harvard Medical School found "the risk of myocardial infarction onset [heart attack] was elevated 4.8 times over baseline in the 60 minutes after marijuana use."[26]

Moreover, French researchers found a connection between marijuana use and heart failure. Reviewing 1,979 medical cases involving marijuana, the researchers found 35 cases of heart-related problems that resulted in nine patient deaths. "Increased reporting of cardiovascular complications related to cannabis and their extreme seriousness (with a death rate of 25.6%) indicate cannabis as a possible risk factor for cardiovascular disease in young adults, in line with previous findings," wrote the researchers. "Given that cannabis is perceived to be harmless by the general public and that legalization of its use is debated, data concerning its danger must be widely disseminated. Practitioners should be aware that cannabis may be a potential triggering factor for cardiovascular complications in young people."[27]

> "Although cannabis smoke is known to contain similar harmful and carcinogenic substances to tobacco smoke, relatively little is understood regarding the respiratory health effects from cannabis smoking."[28]
>
> —Peter Gates et al., researchers at the University of New South Wales Medicine, Sydney, Australia

Effects on the Respiratory System

Because most users smoke marijuana, scientists have also looked for effects of the drug on the respiratory system. "The respiratory health effects from tobacco smoking are well described," wrote a team of scientists at the University of New South Wales Medicine in Sydney, Australia, in 2014. "Cannabis smoke contains a similar profile of carcinogenic chemicals as tobacco smoke but is inhaled

Chronic bronchitis is one of the conditions that has been linked to smoking marijuana. Cannabis smokers also tend to experience more problems with coughing and wheezing than nonsmokers.

more deeply. Although cannabis smoke is known to contain similar harmful and carcinogenic substances to tobacco smoke, relatively little is understood regarding the respiratory health effects from cannabis smoking."[28]

After reviewing the research looking into marijuana and respiratory health, the scientists found evidence linking chronic bronchitis to smoking the drug. "There is consistent evidence that cannabis smoke is associated with inflammation of the airways with an increased visual bronchitis score (diagnosed by bronchoscopic inspection) to a similar magnitude to that which is associated with tobacco smoke," according to the researchers. In addition, smoking marijuana increases the amount of mucous in the airways: "Population-based studies that control for tobacco smoking have consistently reported a higher frequency of cough and sputum production and wheezing among regular cannabis smokers compared with non-smokers." The effects on the airways also make them more prone to infection, the researchers reported. "Data from outpatient medical centres have shown that cannabis-only smokers compared with non-smokers were more likely to enter these services for respiratory illnesses over a 2-year period."[29]

Based on all of the available research about the effects of marijuana on human health, the vast majority of medical professionals believe marijuana is harmful. The American Medical Association (AMA), the largest association of physicians and medical students in the United States, states that "cannabis is a dangerous drug and as such is a public health concern." For this reason, the AMA believes "the sale of cannabis should not be legalized."[30] The American Psychiatric Association (APA), the largest psychiatric organization in the world, concurs. In its *Position Statement on Marijuana as Medicine*, the APA states: "There is no current scientific evidence that marijuana is in any way beneficial for the treatment of any psychiatric disorder. In contrast, current evidence supports, at minimum, a strong association of cannabis use with the onset of psychiatric disorders. Adolescents are particularly vulnerable to harm, given the effects of cannabis on neurological development."[31]

Is Marijuana an Effective Medical Treatment?

CHAPTER

Endocannabinoids (naturally occurring cannabinoids) regulate functions throughout the body. For example, endocannabinoids that attach to receptors in the immune system control the activities of disease-fighting immune cells. Some scientists believe marijuana's cannabinoids can be used to mimic endocannabinoids and stimulate the chemical signaling that fights diseases and relieves some of their symptoms. Marijuana used in this way is known as medical marijuana.

Medical marijuana comes in three basic forms: whole plant, extracts, and synthetic. *Whole plant* refers to the marijuana leaves, flowers, and stems that are smoked or consumed in food or as a tea. *Extracts* refers to individual cannabinoids that are removed from the plant and purified for medical use. *Synthetic* refers to chemical compounds created in a laboratory that are structured like phytocannabinoids or endocannabinoids and act in similar ways within the body.

Some experts and many users of medical marijuana believe whole plant marijuana is more beneficial than extracts and synthetics, because the plant's many ingredients work together to produce a better effect, a process known as synergism. Others disagree, arguing that whole plant marijuana has not been tested in a traditional, clinical fashion, and claims made about its effectiveness are personal, not scientific. Meanwhile, scientists continue to test the effects of marijuana's many compounds, and the process already has yielded several effective medications.

Synthetics for Treating Nausea, Appetite, and Pain

Two forms of medical marijuana have been proven safe and effective, according to the US Food and Drug Administration (FDA), the federal agency charged with approving new drugs in the United States. Those drugs are Marinol and Cesamet. Both are available as capsules to be taken by mouth. The active ingredient in Marinol is a synthetic form of THC, known as dronabinol, while the active ingredient in Cesamet is a synthetic cannabinoid similar to THC, known as nabilone. Both drugs have been approved to treat severe nausea in cancer patients receiving chemotherapy. In its report on Marinol, the FDA stated that the drug was given to 454 patients with cancer, who received a total of 750 courses of treatment of various malignancies. The drug was shown to completely prevent nausea in 33 percent to 36 percent of the patients and to partially reduce the symptoms in 31 percent to 32 percent of the patients.

Marinol also has been approved to treat people with anorexia due to HIV/AIDS. In one study, 139 patients received either Marinol or a capsule with no active ingredients, known as a placebo, for a period of six weeks. "As compared to placebo, Marinol Capsules treatment resulted in a statistically significant improvement in appetite," stated the study's authors. "Trends toward improved body weight and mood, and decreases in nausea were also seen. After completing the study, patients were allowed to continue treatment with Marinol Capsules in an open-label study, in which there was a sustained improvement in appetite."[32]

In addition Marinol has been approved in Denmark to treat symptoms of multiple sclerosis (MS), a disease of the central nervous system that disrupts the flow of information within the brain, and between the brain and body. The drug has been shown to reduce involuntary, or spastic, movements in patients with MS.

Cesamet has been approved by the government of Mexico not only to treat nausea but also to relieve chronic pain. Research performed at the University of Innsbruck in Innsbruck, Austria, found that Cesamet relieved nerve-related pain of MS. Eleven MS patients were given either Cesamet or a placebo. The researchers found that the patients receiving Cesamet "showed a significant decrease of pain."[33]

> "Marinol Capsules treatment resulted in a statistically significant improvement in appetite. Trends toward improved body weight and mood, and decreases in nausea were also seen."[32]
>
> —US Food and Drug Administration, the federal agency that regulates the pharmaceutical industry

Natural Extracts

The first government-approved non-synthetic drug to be made from natural extracts of the hemp plant is Sativex. Approved for

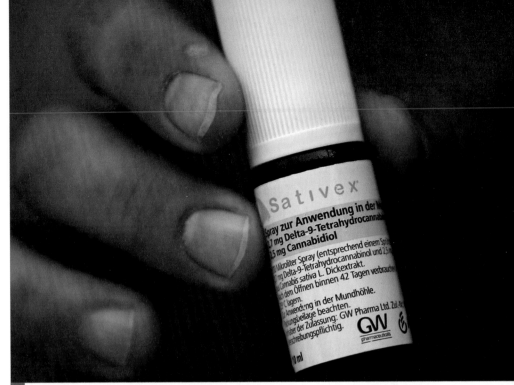

Sativex oral spray (pictured) is the first government-approved non-synthetic drug to be made from natural extracts of the hemp plant. It is used to treat symptoms of multiple sclerosis, an often disabling disease of the central nervous system.

use in the United Kingdom in 2010, Sativex contains two phytocannabinoids: THC and cannabidiol (CBD). Taken as an oral spray, Sativex has been approved in twenty-five countries to treat pain and spasticity in patients with MS. The drug currently is undergoing clinical trials in the United States. In 2014, the FDA put Sativex on its "Fast Track," which the FDA describes as "a process designed to facilitate the development, and expedite the review of drugs to treat serious conditions and fill an unmet medical need."[34]

One of the active extracts in Sativex is CBD, a non-psychoactive compound in marijuana. Since CBD does not produce a "high," some states have approved its use for medical purposes. Although it has not been proven safe and effective by the FDA, a purified oil made from the hemp plant containing large amounts of CBD has shown promise as an antiseizure medication for children. CBD oil is sold in Colorado under the brand name Charlotte's

The Entourage Effect Works

Advocates of medical marijuana say that consuming whole plant marijuana is more beneficial than consuming extracts or synthetic compounds due to what is known as the "entourage effect." NORML, a group that advocates for marijuana legalization, credits the entourage effect for the superior performance of inhaled marijuana over Marinol.

Dronabinol (trade name Marinol) is a legal, synthetic THC alternative to cannabis. Nevertheless, many patients claim they find minimal relief from it, particularly when compared to inhaled marijuana. The active ingredient in Marinol, delta-9-tetrahydrocannabinol, is only one of the compounds isolated in marijuana that appears to be medically beneficial to patients. Other compounds such as cannabidiol (CBD), an anti-convulsant, and cannabichromine (CBC), an anti-inflammatory, are unavailable in Marinol, and patients only have access to their therapeutic properties by using cannabis.

NORML, "FAQs: Why Does Congress Refuse to Reschedule Marijuana to Permit Its Use as a Medicine Under Federal Law?," http://norml.org.

Web. The product was named after Charlotte Figi, a girl with Dravet syndrome, a form of epilepsy. Charlotte was having three hundred grand mal seizures a week—almost two every hour—despite taking traditional antiseizure medications. When Charlotte's parents gave her CBD oil, her seizures nearly stopped. According to her parents, Charlotte went from having twelve hundred seizures a month to four.

Word of the success of CBD oil in reducing childhood epilepsy seizures led other families to try it—with similar results. One was the family of Emily Mirzabegian, a young girl from California who also was diagnosed with Dravet syndrome. Doctors prescribed twelve different medications for Emily, but her seizures continued. Her family tried alternative medicine, including acupuncture, and a ketogenic (mostly fat) diet. Ray Mirzabegian, Emily's father, even took his daughter abroad to receive injections of what were supposed to be tissue-repairing stem cells. Nothing worked. Ray heard about CBD oil on television and decided to give it a try. After taking the hemp plant extract, usually mixed in with her food or a beverage, Emily went from having hundreds of seizures a day to only four a month. Ray was so impressed with CBD oil that he went into business with the makers of Charlotte's Web and began making and selling the product in California.

The Entourage Effect Is Unproven

According to Bertha K. Madras, a professor of psychobiology at Harvard Medical School, the entourage effect has never been proven in clinical trials. She also questions the scientific validity of users' claims about whole plant marijuana's effects, in part because users are under the influence of the drug's psychoactive compounds when they are making their assessments.

> Evidence is needed to prove the validity of the widely held belief and self-reporting that whole plant cannabis is superior to isolated compounds because of synergism [the interaction of discrete agents such that the total effect is greater than the sum of the individual effects] between various components. This is not a trivial issue, as it is a motivating force for whole cannabis plant to be used for medical purposes in lieu of isolated compounds. . . . It is within reason to acknowledge that certain people report relief and symptom improvement while under the influence of cannabis, as corroborated by surveys, case-based studies, anecdotal self-reports, laboratory-based short-term trials. . . . It should be noted that the psychoactive responses engendered by cannabis confound clinical research, as it is a significant obstacle to designing randomized, double-blinded clinical trials.

Bertha K. Madras, *Update of Cannabis and Its Medical Use*. New York: World Health Organization, 2015, pp. 17–18.

Based on these and other reports, the American Epilepsy Society issued a policy statement on CBD and epilepsy:

> The anecdotal reports of positive effects of the marijuana derivative cannabidiol (CBD) for some individuals with treatment-resistant epilepsy give reason for hope. However, we must remember that anecdotal reports alone are not sufficient to support treatment decisions. Robust scientific evidence for the use of marijuana is limited. The lack of information does not mean that marijuana is ineffective for epilepsy. It merely means that we do not know if marijuana is a safe and effective treatment for epilepsy, which is why it should be studied using the well-founded research methods that all other effective treatments for epilepsy have undergone.[35]

Despite the American Epilepsy Society's skepticism, thousands of parents are eager to try CBD oil for their epileptic children. Ray Mirzabegian told *Time* magazine in October 2014 that he had a waiting list of one thousand California families that wanted the CBD oil. The makers of Charlotte's Web in Colorado told *Time* they have a waiting list of twelve thousand families.

Expanded Access to an Antiseizure Medication

Scientific evidence for the use of CBD as an antiseizure medication is now being gathered by the British drug company GW Pharmaceuticals, the makers of Sativex. The company has produced an antiseizure medication called Epidiolex made with purified extracts from the hemp plant. In June 2014, the FDA gave its Fast Track designation for the testing of Epidiolex in the treatment of Dravet syndrome.

While Epidiolex is under clinical review, the FDA is allowing access to the drug through its expanded access program. "FDA understands the interest in making investigational products available to patients while they are being studied for approval, and there are expanded access provisions in both FDA's statute and its regulations to make this possible," stated the FDA in its policy on marijuana. "FDA's expanded-access mechanisms are designed to facilitate the availability of investigational products to patients with serious diseases or conditions when there is no comparable or satisfactory alternative therapy available." The FDA has given doctors at the New York University School of Medicine and University of California, San Francisco, permission to prescribe Epidiolex as an investigational new drug (IND). "There are now 21 active expanded access INDs for Epidiolex treating approximately 300 patients with epilepsy syndromes," stated the FDA in June 2014. "Approximately 95 percent of these INDs are for patients between 1 and 17 years of age."[36]

Protective Effects of CBD

Some scientists reasoned that the same chemical signaling that appears to stop seizures also might blunt the psychoactive effects of THC. To investigate this hypothesis, Raymond J.M. Niesink and Margriet W. van Laar, two researchers at Trimbos Institute in Utrecht, Netherlands, reviewed 1,295 scientific papers that mention CBD. Based on a review of the literature, Niesink and Van Laar concluded: "Studies examining the protective effects of CBD have shown that CBD can counteract the negative effects of THC."[37]

In one of these studies, researchers at the Central Institute of Mental Health in Mannheim, Germany, used brain scans to compare the part of the brain known as the hippocampus in eleven chronic marijuana users and thirteen healthy patients who did not use marijuana. The researchers found that the hippocampus was reduced in size among all the marijuana users but less so among those who had consumed marijuana with higher levels of CBD. This discovery suggests that CBD can protect neurons in the brain. "Lower volume in the right hippocampus in chronic cannabis users was corroborated," wrote the researchers. "Higher THC and lower CBD was associated with this volume reduction indicating neurotoxic effects of THC and neuroprotective effects of CBD."[38]

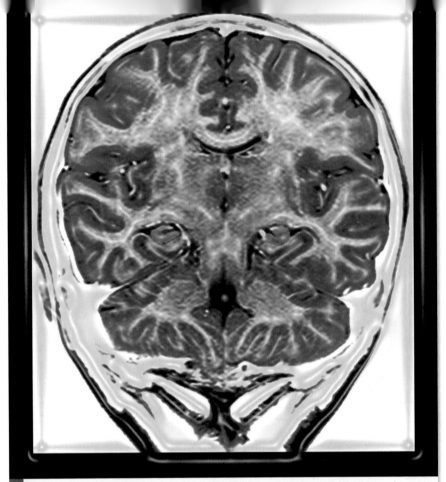

A color-enhanced MRI scan shows a healthy human brain, including the hippocampus (shown as two spots of green). A comparison of brain scans of chronic marijuana users and nonusers has found reduced hippocampus size in the marijuana users.

Treating Anxiety and Psychosis

CBD also appears to reduce anxiety. In one study reviewed by Niesink and Van Laar, healthy volunteers and patients suffering from social anxiety disorder were asked to speak in front of a video camera. Some subjects in each group received CBD, while others received a placebo. "In this experimental situation, CBD was effective in preventing symptoms of anxiety, both in healthy volunteers and in patients with social anxiety disorder,"[39] wrote the researchers.

Since CBD has been shown to decrease anxiety and counteract the effects of THC, researchers wondered if CBD could be used as an antipsychotic medicine. To test this idea, scientists at Heidelberg University in Mannheim, Germany, performed a drug trial on forty-two consenting men and women between the ages of eighteen and fifty who had been diagnosed with schizophrenia. The subjects were patients of the Department of Psychiatry and Psychotherapy of the University of Cologne and were hospitalized throughout the twenty-eight-day trial. The patients received either CBD or the antipsychotic medication amisulpride, which the researchers described as "one of the most effective drugs currently in use for the treatment of schizophrenia." After receiving the drugs for twenty-eight days, the subjects were evaluated.

"Comparison of the clinical effects of amisulpride and cannabidiol [CBD] revealed no relevant difference between the two treatments," stated the researchers. "These results suggest that cannabidiol is as effective at improving psychotic symptoms as the standard antipsychotic amisulpride."[40]

Whole Plant Marijuana

While marijuana extracts and synthetic compounds have been proven to be safe and effective for their intended uses in clinical trials, whole plant marijuana has not. "The FDA has not approved marijuana as a safe and effective drug for any indication,"[41] states the agency. Chuck Rosenberg, the head of the Drug Enforcement Administration, is more direct. "Don't call it medicine—that is a joke," Rosenberg told CBS News. "There are pieces of marijuana—extracts or constituents or component parts—that have great promise, but if you talk about smoking the leaf of marijuana—which is what people are talking about when they talk about medicinal marijuana—it has never been shown to be safe or effective as a medicine."[42]

Before purchasing the drug from a dispensary, medical marijuana users in most states must be diagnosed with a serious

> "Don't call [marijuana] medicine—that is a joke. There are pieces of marijuana—extracts or constituents or component parts—that have great promise, but if you talk about smoking the leaf of marijuana . . . it has never been shown to be safe or effective as a medicine."[42]
>
> —Chuck Rosenberg, the head of the US Drug Enforcement Administration

medical condition, receive a referral from a doctor, and sign up on a patient registry. Among the medical conditions approved by many states for treatment with marijuana are AIDS, anorexia, arthritis, cancer, chronic pain, glaucoma, migraines, seizures, severe nausea, and persistent muscle spasms such as those resulting from MS.

According to a survey conducted by the Public Health Institute (PHI), a nonprofit organization, 320 out of 350—or 91.4 percent—of medical marijuana users said the drug helped with their symptoms. "Five percent of adults in California reported ever using medical marijuana, and most users believed that medical marijuana helped alleviate symptoms or treat a serious medical condition,"[43] stated the report.

Penny Berg Neadeau, a sixty-year-old California woman, is one of the millions of satisfied medical marijuana users. When she was twenty-four, Neadeau suffered a severe lower back injury while

An Oregon woman decides which medical marijuana product to buy. Most states require medical marijuana purchasers to have been diagnosed with a serious medical condition, have a doctor's referral, and sign up on a patient registry.

learning to water-ski. She subsequently had more than twenty procedures to repair the damage and relieve the pain. "My headaches became worse," said Neadeau. "My doctors prescribed every medication on the market—Relpax, Imitrix, Topamax, and Valium. Nothing worked." The headaches became so bad that Neadeau had to quit her job. "I had no social life, I stopped driving, and I could no longer paint or garden, my favorite activities," Neadeau recalled. A close friend who used medical marijuana suggested Neadeau try it. Neadeau was skeptical, in part because her daughter was a drug addict who died in 2015 from drug-related causes. "As the mother of someone who lost her life because of drugs, I had an extremely hard time considering using marijuana, even for medicinal purposes," said Neadeau. Nonetheless, feeling she had "nothing left to lose" after her daughter's death, Neadeau got a doctor's prescription for medical marijuana for her migraines, bought a marijuana cookie, and took a single bite. "At first I felt no effect," she explained. "However, playing with the dosage, I found the right amount for me. With the medical marijuana, I have a life again. And unlike other medications, the cookies have no side effects other than some sleepiness. I still have mixed feelings about taking a 'street drug' . . . however, I feel quite strongly that there are wonderful properties with medicinal marijuana, just as there can be terrible effects if used improperly."[44]

> "With the medical marijuana, I have a life again. . . . I feel quite strongly that there are wonderful properties with medicinal marijuana, just as there can be terrible effects if used improperly."[44]
>
> —Penny Berg Neadeau, a medical marijuana user

Critics of medical marijuana laws suggest that many people are obtaining the drug for recreational purposes rather than for medical needs. "The general feeling in the law enforcement community is that California's medical marijuana law is a giant con job,"[45] said John Lovell, a lobbyist for narcotics officers, police chiefs, and correctional supervisors. The authors of the PHI study say their research refutes this charge:

Our study contradicts commonly held beliefs that medical marijuana is being overused by healthy individuals. . . . It is clear that [the medical marijuana law] is helping people who are sick and use medical marijuana to treat serious medical conditions, including cancer, migraines and chronic pain, to manage their symptoms. Medical marijuana is not solely being used by young men who are accessing medical marijuana under the pretence that they have a serious medical condition and that they "need" medical marijuana to treat it.[46]

Although noteworthy, the PHI study is hardly conclusive. For one thing, the group surveyed is small: Only 350 people out of the more than 1 million estimated medical marijuana users in California were questioned about their experiences. In addition, common sense suggests that people who are obtaining medical marijuana under false pretenses are not going to admit that fact in a survey, nor are they going to say that the drug is not working.

To further complicate the issue, the subjects of the PHI survey were assessing their experiences while under the influence of a psychoactive drug. "The doses at which marijuana produces euphoria almost fully overlap with its putative therapeutic effects. Accordingly it is difficult to separate the two," writes Bertha K. Madras, a professor of psychobiology at Harvard Medical School. "The gold standard of therapeutics is to develop drugs that alleviate specific symptoms without interfering with or compromising brain function."[47]

Without such clinical trials, whole plant marijuana will not be approved by the FDA as safe and effective. Nevertheless, millions of Americans will continue to experiment with medical marijuana to relieve symptoms of serious medical conditions for which there are no other effective treatments.

> "It is clear that [the medical marijuana law] is helping people who are sick and use medical marijuana to treat serious medical conditions, including cancer, migraines and chronic pain, to manage their symptoms."[46]
>
> —Public Health Institute (PHI), a nonprofit organization that studies health issues

4 CHAPTER
Does Marijuana Use Lead to Drug Abuse?

Marijuana is classified by the US federal government as a drug. Before a drug can be used legally in the United States, it must be approved by the FDA, which, by law, must find that the drug not only is effective, but also safe. When analyzing drug safety, the FDA looks at several things, including the drug's "actual or relative potential for abuse; . . . its history or current pattern of abuse; . . . the scope, duration, and significance of abuse; . . . what, if any, risk there is to the public health; . . . [and] its psychic or physiological dependence liability,"[48] according to physican Douglas C. Throckmorton. Proponents of marijuana legalization say that marijuana's potential for abuse is lower than for other legal drugs, including alcohol and nicotine. Critics of marijuana legalization disagree. They say that marijuana has a high risk for abuse and that its use often leads to the use of other illegal and addictive drugs.

A High Potential for Abuse

In the nineteenth century marijuana was listed in both the British and American drug manuals, known as Pharmacopeia, as a sedative and an anticonvulsant medication. By 1941, marijuana had been removed from both the British and US Pharmacopeia. Since people use different techniques when smoking marijuana, the amounts of THC they consume—the doses—can vary from person to person. This makes it impossible to control and recommend dosages. In addition, medical professionals noted that marijuana had a high risk of abuse. In 1970, the US Congress passed the Controlled Substances Act (CSA), which lists marijuana on its Schedule I along with heroin, cocaine, and other narcotics as a drug with no currently accepted medical use and a high potential for abuse. Critics of the CSA believe that marijuana does not belong on Schedule I. "It is doubtful that marijuana is addictive in any meaningful sense," wrote Paul Armentano, a senior policy analyst for NORML. "Although a small percentage of marijuana users may find quitting difficult, this does not justify putting it in the same legal category as heroin."[49]

The National Institutes of Health (NIH) disagrees. "Marijuana use can lead to the development of problem use, known as a marijuana use disorder, which in severe cases takes the form of addiction,"[50] states the organization. The NIH bases its position on the findings of the APA. The 2013 edition of the organization's classification and diagnostic tool, *Diagnostic and Statistical Manual of Mental Disorders,* states: "People who regularly use cannabis can develop all the general diagnostic features of a substance use disorder."[51]

The chapter lists eleven symptoms of cannabis use disorder, including such things as "Cannabis is often taken in larger amounts or over a longer period than was intended," "There is a persistent desire or unsuccessful efforts to cut down or control cannabis use," and "Cannabis is taken to relieve or avoid withdrawal symptoms."[52] A person with two or three of the symptoms is said to have a mild disorder, while a person with four to five symptoms has a moderate disorder, and a person with six or more symptoms has a severe disorder. The manual goes on to outline some of the signs of the disorder:

> **"People who regularly use cannabis can develop all the general diagnostic features of a substance use disorder."[51]**
>
> —American Psychiatric Association, the largest psychiatric organization in the world

People with a cannabis use disorder may use cannabis throughout the day for periods of months or years and may spend many hours a day under its influence. Others may use less frequently but still experience use-related problems. Use of cannabis at home may lead to arguments with spouses or parents, and its use in the presence of children can adversely impact family functioning. Use of cannabis on the job or while working at a job that requires drug testing can be a sign of a cannabis use disorder. Those who continue using despite knowledge of physical or psychological problems show evidence of a disorder.[53]

Quitting marijuana use is not as easy as Armentano suggests, according to the APA. "The abrupt cessation of daily or near-daily cannabis use often results in the onset of cannabis withdrawal syndrome," states the APA manual. The symptoms of marijuana withdrawal can be severe enough to cause the user to go back to the drug. As the APA states, a sudden stop in marijuana use "often results and contributes to difficulty quitting or relapse among those trying to abstain."[54]

Measuring the Risk of Dependence

While advocates of marijuana legalization agree that some marijuana users can develop cannabis use disorder, they say the risk of forming a dependence on the drug is very low. "According to the Institute of Medicine's [IOM] 267-page report, fewer than 10 percent of those who try cannabis ever meet the clinical criteria for a diagnosis of 'drug dependence.' By contrast, the IOM reported that 32 percent of tobacco users, 23 percent of heroin users, 17 percent of cocaine users and 15 percent of alcohol users meet the criteria for 'drug dependence,'"[55] writes Armentano.

Like cocaine (pictured) and heroin, marijuana is classified by federal law as a Schedule I drug. Drugs in this classification are listed as having a high potential for abuse and no currently acceptable medical use.

Marijuana Is Not Toxic

NORML, an organization that lobbies for an end to marijuana prohibition, states that marijuana is not toxic, no matter how much is consumed.

Marijuana is far less dangerous than alcohol or tobacco. It fails to inflict the types of serious health consequences these two legal drugs cause. According to a recent World Health Organization report alcohol consumption is linked to four percent of all deaths worldwide. Similarly, more than 400,000 deaths each year are attributed to tobacco smoking. By comparison, marijuana is nontoxic and cannot cause death by overdose. . . . The negative consequences primarily associated with marijuana—such as an arrest or jail time—are the result of the criminal prohibition of cannabis, not the use of marijuana itself.

NORML, "FAQs: Don't Alcohol and Tobacco Use Already Cause Enough Damage to Society? Why Should We Legalize Another Intoxicant?," http://norml.org.

Although these figures are accurate, they are somewhat misleading, because the percentage is based on the total number of people who have ever tried marijuana. According to a 2015 Gallup poll, 44 percent of American adults said they had tried marijuana at some time in their lives—approximately 100 million people. This figure includes tens of millions who tried the drug once and never used it again. A more relevant statistic is the percentage of people who used the drug within the past year and then went on to develop marijuana use disorder. According to a 2015 study conducted by researchers at Columbia University in New York, that percentage is three times higher than the one Armentano suggested. "While not all marijuana users experience problems, nearly 3 of 10 marijuana users manifested a marijuana use disorder,"[56] wrote the researchers. The odds are even higher for people who use the drug every day. The 2012 National Survey on Drug Use and Health found that up to 50 percent of daily marijuana smokers become addicted.

As with psychosis, brain damage, and suicide, the risks of developing marijuana use disorder are greatest for people who start using marijuana as teenagers. "Those who begin using the drug in their teens have approximately a one in six [17 percent] risk of developing dependence,"[57] states the United Nations Office on Drugs and Crime. Researchers at the University of Minnesota agree. They found that people who begin using marijuana before age eighteen are four to seven times more likely to develop a marijuana use disorder than those who started using the drug as adults. "We obtained significantly elevated odds ratios (OR) for a cannabis use disorder at each of teenage years (ages 12–18), when compared to older recent onset users (aged 22–26),"[58] stated the authors of the study.

Increased Mortality Rate

Marijuana use disorder can be deadly, according to a 2012 study conducted by researchers at the Centre for Addiction and Mental

Marijuana Can Be Toxic

In 2014 researchers in Germany documented the first known cases of people dying from marijuana overdoses in a study published in *Forensic Science International*.

> The acute toxicity of cannabinoids is said to be low and there is little public awareness of the potentially hazardous cardiovascular effects of cannabis, e.g. marked increase in heart rate or supine blood pressure. We describe the cases of two young, putative healthy men who died unexpectedly under the acute influence of cannabinoids. To our knowledge, these are the first cases of suspected fatal cannabis intoxications where full postmortem investigations, including autopsy, toxicological, histological, immunohistochemical and genetical examinations, were carried out. After exclusion of other causes of death we assume that the young men experienced fatal cardiovascular complications evoked by smoking cannabis.

Benno Hartung et al., "Sudden Unexpected Death Under Acute Influence of Cannabis," *Forensic Science International*, April 2014, p. e11.

VIEWPOINT

Health in Toronto, Canada. The researchers studied the records of 819,489 individuals hospitalized in California with various substance use disorders between 1990 and 2005. They followed the subjects for up to sixteen years to see how many had died from any cause. After adjusting for standard age, gender, and race, the researchers found that people with marijuana use disorder had a mortality rate 3.85 times higher than that of the general population. This rate was higher than the mortality rates for those with cocaine use disorder (2.96) and alcohol use disorder (3.83), although lower than the rates for those with opioid (opiates such as heroin) use disorder (5.71) or methamphetamine use disorder (4.67). "Given the lack of long-term cohort studies of mortality risk among individuals with methamphetamine-related disorders, as well as among those with cocaine- or cannabis-related conditions, the current study provides important information for the assessment of the comparative drug-related burden associated with use and addiction,"[59] stated the researchers.

Critics of the Centre for Addiction and Mental Health study point out that while it shows a higher death rate for people treated for marijuana use disorder, it does not show that marijuana caused the deaths through drug-related medical conditions. It is more likely, they contend, that the deaths are related to the drug being illegal rather than to its use being dangerous. Since recreational marijuana is illegal in most states, buying it can bring the user into contact with criminals, and this can be dangerous. "I know the dark side," wrote Susan Shapiro, author of the memoir *Lighting Up*. "I was addicted for 27 years. After starting to smoke weed at Bob Dylan concerts when I was 13, I saw how it can make you say and do things that are provocative and perilous. I bought pot in bad neighborhoods at 3 a.m., confronted a dealer for selling me a dime bag of oregano, let shady pushers I barely knew deliver marijuana, like pizza, to my home."[60] Advocates for marijuana legalization say that if the drug were legal, the death rate of marijuana users would go down, because they would not be drawn into the criminal web.

The Gateway Sequence

Marijuana may be less addictive than heroin and methamphetamine, but many people believe it presents another danger: It

A user prepares his heroin fix. Many studies show that marijuana is a gateway drug—meaning it leads to use of more-addictive drugs, including heroin and methamphetamine.

leads to the abuse of other, harder drugs. This phenomenon, known as the "gateway sequence," was first documented in a study of New York high school students in 1975. The study found that "26 percent of marijuana users progress to LSD, amphetamines, or heroin," while "only 1 percent of nondrug users and 4 percent of legal drug users do so." The study's author concluded: "Marijuana . . . is a crucial step in the way to other illicit drugs."[61]

Several other studies have found similar results, including a 2015 research project at Columbia University in New York involving 43,093 individuals aged eighteen years and older. The researchers found that 44.7 percent of marijuana users went on to use other illicit drugs. "According to the gateway hypothesis, individuals rarely use certain substances, such as heroin or cocaine, without having first used 'gateway' substances, such as legal drugs or cannabis," wrote the researchers. "The validity of the gateway hypothesis has been the topic of intense debate since the early 1970s. Although some studies have found that use of legal drugs or cannabis are not a requirement for the progression to other illicit drugs, most studies have supported the 'gateway sequence.'"[62]

Subsequent research contends that marijuana use not only precedes the use of harder drugs, but it also increases the chances of the user abusing other drugs, even legal ones, such as alcohol. In 2016, researchers at Albert Einstein College of Medicine in the Bronx, New York, studied 29,582 individuals who responded to two surveys. The researchers found that adults who were using marijuana at the time of the first survey were more than five times more likely than nonusers to have an alcohol use disorder (AUD) three years later, when the second survey was taken. In addition, those marijuana users who already had an alcohol use disorder at the time of the first survey had a greater risk of their alcohol use disorder worsening. "Cannabis use is associated with increased risk of AUD onset and persistence over the course of three years among U.S. adults,"[63] wrote Andrea Weinberger, the lead author of the study.

Seeking Stronger Effects

While belief in the gateway sequence is well established, experts disagree about its cause. Some people believe marijuana use leads to further drug use because the users become used to the drug's

Because alcohol is legal, consumers can shop for wine, beer, or liquor without being urged to buy more dangerous substances. Advocates of legalized marijuana envision a similar scenario: If marijuana were legal, purchasers would not be confronted by dealers urging them to buy stronger drugs.

effects and begin to crave greater stimulation. These experts point to research conducted at the University of Cagliari, in Monserrato, Italy, that studied the effects of cannabinoids on rat brains. "Recent studies have raised concerns about subtle, long-lasting neurobiological changes that might be triggered by exposure to cannabis derivatives, especially in a critical phase of brain maturation, such as puberty," wrote the researchers. They gave cannabinoids known as WIN to both adolescent and adult rats for three days. Two weeks later, they administered WIN to rats that had received the drug and also to others that had not. The researchers found that the rats that had been pretreated with cannabinoids released much less of the reward chemical dopamine (DA) than did the rats that had never before received the drug. This suggested that the pretreated rats had built up a tolerance to the drug and were not experiencing a strong reaction to it. "In cannabinoid-administered rats, DA neurons were significantly less responsive to the stimulating action of WIN, regardless of the age of pretreatment,"[64] wrote the researchers. Commenting on this study, the NIH stated, "To the extent that these findings generalize to humans, this could help explain the increased vulnerability for addiction to other substances of abuse later in life that most epidemiological studies have reported for people who begin marijuana use early in life."[65]

> "There is no conclusive evidence that the effects of marijuana are causally linked to the subsequent use of other illicit drugs."[66]
>
> —NORML, an organization working toward the legalization of marijuana use for adults

Some experts, however, dispute the findings of the University of Cagliari study. "Preliminary animal studies alleging that marijuana 'primed' the brain for other drug-taking behavior have not been replicated, nor are they supported by epidemiological human data," states NORML. "There is no conclusive evidence that the effects of marijuana are causally linked to the subsequent use of other illicit drugs."[66]

Pathways to Other Drugs

Getting used to the drug and seeking a better "high" is just one of many forces that drives the gateway sequence. "Several complementary pathways involving biochemical, social learning and environmental factors may contribute to explain the progression from cannabis use to other illicit drug use," wrote the authors of the 2015 Columbia University study of the gateway sequence. They explain:

> Cannabis users are often more exposed to opportunities to use other illicit drugs because the environment and distribution channels for cannabis and other illegal drugs frequently overlap. Cannabis use also provides the individual with learning experiences (e.g., pleasurable effects) that can encourage experimentation with other illicit drugs. Furthermore, the pharmacological effects of cannabis appear to lead to neuroadaptations that render the brain more sensitive to the euphoric effects of other illicit drugs. Being intoxicated with one drug may also lower reservations about using other drugs.[67]

As the study points out, users of marijuana often come into contact with dealers who sell not only marijuana, but also harder drugs. Since drug dealers make more money selling harder drugs, they often encourage marijuana buyers to purchase higher-priced narcotics. However, advocates for legalizing marijuana point out that this occurs because buying marijuana is illegal. "When you go to a liquor store for a bottle of wine, there isn't a person there trying to sell you cocaine or other dangerous products," said Morgan Fox, a spokesperson for Marijuana Policy Project, an advocacy group. "An illegal narcotics dealer has incentive to push dangerous drugs."[68]

Advocates of marijuana legalization suggest that making the drug legal would remove several of the social learning and environmental factors that contribute to the gateway sequence, such as bringing the marijuana into contact with narcotics dealers, receiving encouragement to try harder drugs, and lowering reservations about using other drugs. As leaders and voters in various states consider legalizing marijuana, researchers will be watching Colorado in particular, since it has legalized both the use and sale of marijuana, to see if legalization has any effect—good or bad—on the prevalence of marijuana use disorder and the gateway sequence.

5 CHAPTER

Should Marijuana Be Decriminalized?

The legal status of marijuana use varies from state to state within the United States. Forty-one of the fifty states allow the medical use of marijuana, with twenty-four allowing the use of the whole plant for medical purposes and seventeen allowing the use of CBD extracts and synthetic cannabinoids. Four of the twenty-four states that allow the use of whole plant marijuana for medical purposes—Colorado, Alaska, Washington, and Oregon—also allow its use for recreational purposes, as does the District of Columbia. Several other states are considering legalizing the use of marijuana for all purposes. Advocates of legalization are calling for an end to marijuana prohibition. Others urge caution, suggesting there might be lessons to learn from the states that have legalized the drug. Others oppose legalization altogether, saying sufficient evidence already shows marijuana use is harmful to individuals and society.

The Lure of Money

One of the main reasons business and government leaders favor legalization is potential profit. Legalizing marijuana takes cash out of the pockets of criminals and puts it into the hands of legitimate businesses. "[Marijuana sales] is more and more being seen as a legitimate business, and now we hope businesses can come out of the shadows,"[69] said Rob Bonta, a California state assemblyman.

> "[Marijuana sales] is more and more being seen as a legitimate business, and now we hope businesses can come out of the shadows."[69]
>
> —Rob Bonta, a California state assemblyman

The boost to a state's economy can be huge. For example, sales of medical marijuana in California totaled $2.7 billion in 2015. According to ArcView and New Frontier, two marijuana research firms, that figure could double to $5.4 billion by 2020 if California voters legalize recreational marijuana.

The sale of marijuana is not the only source of economic activity when the drug becomes legal. The businesses that sell marijuana contribute to the economic boom by spending money, buying or renting property, building or refurbishing stores, hiring people, and advertising. "It's a huge opportunity for everybody," said Meg Sanders, chief executive officer (CEO) of Mindful, a Colorado marijuana dispensary. "There's this whole ancillary side of security teams and marketing teams and packaging and you name it that comes along with this, not to mention the huge boost to the economy that we've done in particular to contractors, HVAC, plumbers. It's massive."[70]

The legalization of marijuana in Colorado fueled a boom in commercial real estate, according to Kelly Brough, president of the Denver Metro Chamber of Commerce. "The operations that grow marijuana utilize often underutilized commercial, industrial big warehouses," said Brough. "These tend to be less expensive commercial space. We saw the price for those go up for those spaces when marijuana was legalized."[71]

Hundreds of New Yorkers rally in 2016 for marijuana legalization. At present, only four states (Colorado, Alaska, Washington, and Oregon) and the District of Columbia allow recreational use of marijuana.

Benefits to Government

Legalization of marijuana creates a windfall of new tax revenues for state and local governments. The state of Colorado charges 27.9 percent in sales taxes on recreational marijuana, including a 2.9 percent retail and medical marijuana sales tax, a 10 percent retail marijuana special sales tax, and a 15 percent marijuana excise tax.

In addition, marijuana businesses must pay the state retail/medical marijuana application and license fees. They also pay property tax on properties they purchase or rent to launch or grow their businesses. Like other Colorado businesses marijuana dispensaries pay a 4.63 percent tax on their net income.

According to state officials, Colorado took in $58.7 million in tax revenue from marijuana sales taxes in 2014, the first year the drug was commercially available. The new revenue was a benefit for the state, but it fell far short of the $100 million the office of Colorado governor John Hickenlooper had forecast the state would gain from marijuana sales. However, the next year more than made up for the shortfall. According to the Colorado Department of Revenue, the state took in $135 million in marijuana taxes and fees on sales of $996,184,788 worth of recreational and medical cannabis in 2015. "I attribute [the boom in marijuana sales] to . . . more and more people . . . comfortable with the legalization of marijuana," said Tyler Henson, president of the Colorado Cannabis Chamber of Commerce, an organization dedicated to the economic advancement of the cannabis industry. "They don't see it as something that's bad for them."[72]

> "I attribute [the boom in marijuana sales] to . . . more and more people . . . comfortable with the legalization of marijuana. They don't see it as something that's bad for them."[72]
>
> —Tyler Henson, president of the Colorado Cannabis Chamber of Commerce

Decreasing the Cost of Drug Enforcement

Proponents of marijuana legalization say that not only will state and local governments gain tax revenues when the drug is legal, but they also will save money. Marijuana advocates suggest law enforcement will spend less time investigating and arresting marijuana dealers and users, the courts will spend less time handling

Legalization Has Damaged the Mexican Drug Cartels

Proponents of marijuana legalization believe the best way to defeat the Mexican drug cartels that supply marijuana to the United States is not by prosecuting a "war on drugs," but by legalizing the drug. Journalist Ioan Grillo reports that US authorities have already noted a drop in cross-border trade.

Agents on the 2,000 mile–U.S. border have wrestled with . . . smuggling techniques for decades, seemingly unable to stop the northward flow of drugs and southward flow of dollars and guns. But the amount of one drug—marijuana—seems to have finally fallen. US Border Patrol has been seizing steadily smaller quantities of the drug, from 2.5 million pounds in 2011 to 1.9 million pounds in 2014. Mexico's army has noted an even steeper decline, confiscating 664 tons of cannabis in 2014, a drop of 32% compared to year before. This fall appears to have little to do with law enforcement, however, and all to do with the wave of US marijuana legalization.

Ioan Grillo, "US Legalization of Marijuana Has Hit Mexican Cartels' Cross-Border Trade," *Time*, April 8, 2015. www.time.com.

marijuana cases, and probation officers will spend less time overseeing the activities of those convicted of violating marijuana laws. The reduced caseloads will allow the government to use fewer people or at least not expand as rapidly as they would were marijuana to remain illegal.

According to the Drug Policy Alliance, an organization working to reform the nation's drug laws, this is exactly what has happened in Colorado. Arrests for the possession, cultivation, and distribution of marijuana decreased 95 percent after the state legalized the recreational use of marijuana, falling from 39,027 cases in 2011 to just 2,036 cases in 2014. "Those 37,000 fewer cases represent a savings of untold millions of dollars in court costs and law enforcement fees," wrote Christopher Ingraham, a blogger with the *Washington Post*. "They represent countless police man-hours able to be devoted to other tasks."[73]

Relatively few people are sent to prison for possessing marijuana. Those convicted on marijuana possession charges often were arrested for another reason and happened to have marijuana on them at the time. Once the arresting officers confiscate the marijuana, it is easy to prove guilt for this offense. However, some people are arrested with large amounts of marijuana in their possession—probably to sell illegally—and are sent to prison. Keeping them in prison is costly. Once marijuana

Legalization Has Not Damaged the Mexican Drug Cartels

Many experts believe that legalizing marijuana would weaken the drug cartels. Journalist Keegan Hamilton argues that the gangs are far too entrenched in the trade to be booted out by legalization.

> If legal pot remains the law of the land, it is widely assumed that Mexican drug cartels will be out several billion dollars in annual revenue. But talk to entrepreneurs familiar with the existing marijuana industry in Washington and Colorado—and to law enforcement agents who deal with gang crime—and there is reason for skepticism. Mexican drug traffickers are undoubtedly active in Washington and Colorado. . . . Joe Gagliardi, a gang-unit detective in Seattle's county sheriff's office, says, "I just don't see the legislation of marijuana causing any problems for the criminals. The gangs are still going to grow marijuana and they're still going to sell marijuana, only now it will be legal for them to walk around with an ounce supply individually packaged and not have any repercussions."

Keegan Hamilton, "Why Legalizing Pot Won't Curb the Drug War," *Atlantic*, December 3, 2012. www.theatlantic.com.

is legal, the elimination of marijuana-related prison sentences will reduce prison overcrowding and save money, marijuana advocates argue. In addition, they maintain that keeping marijuana violators out of prison will prevent those criminals—often young and nonviolent—from meeting other, more dangerous criminals and becoming involved with them, their associates, or their gangs after being released.

Legalization and Crime

Those who support marijuana legalization suggest that not only will marijuana-related arrests plummet, but the overall crime rate will also drop once the drug is legalized. Since marijuana users can purchase the drug legally, they will avoid mixing in the criminal environment where the drug currently circulates. This, in turn, will cut down on the use of stronger drugs. On the seller side, drug dealers often clash over their distribution areas, or turf. Legalization of marijuana might reduce "turf wars" and other drug-related violence.

Such positive outcomes have yet to materialize, though. According to the Colorado Bureau of Investigation, the overall crime rate has not fallen since recreational marijuana use was legalized in the state. On the contrary, the crime rate has risen dramatically. According to the bureau's 2014 Crime in Colorado report, the statewide crime rate—based on the number of arrests—increased 21 percent from 2012 to 2014. This followed a nine-year decline in the state's crime rate, from 1,300 arrests per 100,000 people in 2004 to just 857 arrests per 100,000 people in 2012. After recreational marijuana was legalized, the arrest rate soared to 1,037 arrests per 100,000 people in 2014. There is no proof that marijuana legalization caused the increased crime rate, but while arrest rates were rising 9 percent from 2013 to 2014 in Colorado, they are declining across the rest of the United States, according to the Federal Bureau of Investigation (FBI). "Two-year arrest trends show violent crime arrests declined 0.8 percent in 2014 when compared with 2013 arrests, and property crime arrests decreased 2.7 percent when compared with 2013 arrests,"[74] states the FBI.

An increase in the overall crime rate also has been observed in Washington State. The Seattle Police Department reported that the number of property crimes has increased since marijuana possession became legal in December 2012. In 2012, the number of property crimes in Seattle stood at slightly more than 32,000. By 2013 the number had risen to 36,815—a 15 percent increase. In 2014, the number of property crimes rose another 10 percent to 40,666—27 percent higher than in 2012. These figures also ran counter to national trends. The FBI reported the number of property crimes declined 4.3 percent nationwide from 2013 to 2014.

Drivers Under the Influence

Since driving under the influence of marijuana is already illegal, proponents of legalization suggest it would be unlikely that legalizing marijuana will increase the number of driving-under-the-influence (DUI) arrests or driving-related crimes. In fact, with marijuana use out in the open, anti–drunk driving techniques—such

A wrecked car is loaded onto a truck for removal after a crash that left four people dead in New York. The driver had smoked marijuana before getting behind the wheel. Marijuana-related car crashes have increased in states that have legalized the drug.

as having a designated driver—might be adopted to caution users, and these might actually reduce DUI arrests and automobile accidents related to marijuana.

Early evidence from the state of Washington, however, suggests this is not the case. Fatal accidents involving drivers who had recently used marijuana more than doubled the year after the state legalized recreational marijuana. Marijuana use was involved in 17 percent of fatal traffic accidents in 2014, up from 8 percent in 2013, the year before recreational marijuana was legalized in Washington. "The significant increase in fatal crashes involving marijuana is alarming," said Peter Kissinger, CEO of AAA Foundation for Traffic Safety, a nonprofit organization that funds traffic safety research. "Washington serves as an eye-opening case study for what other states may experience with road safety after legalizing the drug."[75]

> "The significant increase in fatal crashes involving marijuana is alarming. Washington serves as an eye-opening case study for what other states may experience with road safety after legalizing the drug."[75]
>
> —Peter Kissinger, CEO of AAA Foundation for Traffic Safety, a nonprofit organization that funds traffic safety research

Colorado also saw a sharp increase in marijuana-related traffic fatalities after recreational marijuana was legalized, according to a report by the Rocky Mountain High Intensity Drug Trafficking Area (RMHIDTA), part of the federal government's Office of National Drug Control Policy. "The average number of marijuana-related traffic deaths increased 41 percent in the two years recreational marijuana was legalized (2013–2014) compared to the medical marijuana commercialization years (2009–2012)," states the report. More than 19 percent of all traffic deaths in Colorado were marijuana-related in 2014, compared to 14.76 percent in 2013. "In 2014, when retail marijuana stores began operating, there was a 32 percent increase in marijuana-related traffic deaths in just one year,"[76] wrote the authors of the report.

The Human Cost of Legalization

The human cost of marijuana legalization was not confined to automobile crashes. The number of marijuana-related hospitalizations and emergency room visits also have increased since Colorado legalized marijuana. "In the three years after medical marijuana was commercialized, compared to the three years prior, there was a 46 percent increase in hospitalization related to marijuana," stated the RMHIDTA report. Much of that increase occurred in the first year after businesses could sell marijuana. "In 2014, when retail marijuana businesses began operating, there was a 38 percent increase in the number of marijuana-related hospitalizations in only one year,"[77] states the RMHIDTA report. Marijuana-related emergency room visits increased 29 percent in 2014 as well.

Marijuana use affects not only traffic safety but also workplace safety, according to the National Institute on Drug Abuse. Researchers studying drug-tested federal employees found that those who tested positive for marijuana use on a preemployment drug test had 55 percent more industrial accidents and 85 percent more injuries than those who tested negative for marijuana use. If those accident and injury rates remain the same in states legalizing marijuana, the effects will be devastating, because the number of employees testing positive for marijuana rose after Colorado and Washington legalized the drug. According to a 2014 study by Quest Diagnostics, a clinical laboratory corporation, positive test rates for marijuana use among workers in Colorado increased 20 percent in 2013, the first year that recreational marijuana was legal. Positive rates for the drug increased 23 percent in Washington the same year. Those rates are three to four times higher than the national average of just 6.2 percent for this period.

Less Perceived Risk

A major concern of marijuana legalization critics has been that making the drug legal will lower the perceived risk of using the drug among young people. "For youth and young adults, more permissive cannabis regulations correlate with decreases in the perceived risk of use,"[78] stated the UNODC's *World Drug Report 2014*. The Institute for Social Research at the University of Michigan substantiated these findings in its *Monitoring the Future: National Survey Results on Drug Use 1975–2015*. For several years, beginning in 2001, the percentage of students who saw "a great risk" in using marijuana "regularly" rose. However, when medical marijuana was legalized by several states in 2011, the perceived risk began to fall. After four states legalized recreational marijuana, perceived risk dropped even further. "Perceived risk of smoking marijuana regularly declined in all three grades [8, 10, and 12], significantly so in 12th grade," states the *Monitoring the Future* report. "In all three grades, the percentage seeing great risk of smoking marijuana regularly is at the lowest point ever recorded in the study—58%, 43%, and 32% in grades 8, 10, and 12, respectively."[79]

Opponents of marijuana legalization worry that less concern about the drug's dangers would lead to more use among young people. Early data from Colorado seemed to contradict this idea. According to the Healthy Kids Colorado Survey conducted by the state of Colorado, the number of high school students who admitted to using marijuana declined in 2013—the first year the drug was legal for adults in the state. According to the survey, 20

Hospital emergency rooms in Colorado are seeing more patients with marijuana-related problems now than they did before the drug was legalized. Hospitalizations are also on the rise for health problems resulting from marijuana use.

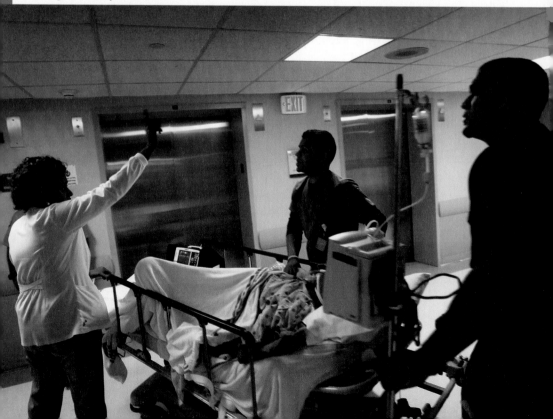

percent of high school students admitted using marijuana in 2013 compared to 22 percent in 2011—a decline of 2 percent. The number of students who said they had tried marijuana at some point in their lives also declined 2 percent, from 39 percent in 2011 to 37 percent in 2013. Marijuana legalization advocates celebrated the news. "Once again, claims that regulating marijuana would leave Colorado in ruins have proven to be unfounded," declared Mason Tvert, a spokesperson for the Marijuana Policy Project, a marijuana advocacy group. "How many times do marijuana prohibition supporters need to be proven wrong before they stop declaring our marijuana laws are increasing teen use?"[80]

The celebration was premature. Research conducted by the federal government two years later found marijuana use among teens in Colorado had not declined since legalization; it had surged. "In the two year average (2013/2014) since Colorado legalized recreational marijuana, youth past month marijuana use increased 20 percent compared to the two year average prior to legalization (2011/2012)," stated a 2016 report by the RMHIDTA. Once again, the Colorado experience ran counter to national trends. "Nationally youth past month marijuana use declined 4 percent during the same time,"[81] added the report.

> "For youth and young adults, more permissive cannabis regulations correlate with decreases in the perceived risk of use."[78]
>
> —*World Drug Report 2014*, a publication of the United Nations Office on Drugs and Crime

The increase in marijuana use among teens made Colorado the nation's leader in youth marijuana use. "The latest 2013/2014 results show Colorado youth ranked #1 in the nation for past month marijuana use, up from #4 in 2011/2012,"[82] stated the RMHIDTA. In fact, past-month marijuana use for Colorado adolescents in 2013–2014 was 74 percent higher than the national average for the same period.

Weighing the Benefits and Hazards

The point of legalizing marijuana for recreational purposes is to allow more adults to use the drug for pleasure. Scientific evidence suggests that increased use of marijuana among adults will be accompanied by increases in cannabis use disorder, memory loss, and respiratory problems. In addition, increased use among adults has been accompanied by increased use among young people. Considering the harmful effects of marijuana on the structure of the developing brains of adolescents as well as the proven links between teen use of marijuana and the onset of marijuana use disorder, anxiety disorders, psychosis, schizophrenia, and suicide, voters and leaders must decide if the pleasure for some is worth the harm to others.

Introduction: The World's Illicit Drug of Choice

1. International Narcotics Control Board, *Report of the International Narcotics Control Board for 2013* (E/INCB/2013/1). New York: United Nations, 2014, p. 93.
2. Madeline H. Meier et al., "Persistent Cannabis Users Show Neuropsychological Decline from Childhood to Midlife," *Proceedings of the National Academy of Sciences of the United States of America*, August 27, 2012, p. E2657. www.pnas.org.
3. Quoted in Abigail Sullivan Moore, "This Is Your Brain on Drugs," *New York Times*, October 29, 2014. www.nytimes.com.
4. National Institutes of Health, *NIDA Research Report Series: Marijuana*. Washington, DC: US Department of Health and Human Services, 2016, p. 2.
5. United Nations Office on Drugs and Crime, *World Drug Report 2014*. New York: United Nations, 2014, p. 44.

Chapter 1: What Are the Facts?

6. United Nations Office on Drugs and Crime, *World Drug Report 2015*. New York: United Nations, 2015, p. 13.
7. Department of Economic and Social Affairs of the United Nations Secretariat, *World Youth Report 2003*. New York: United Nations, 2003, p. 149.
8. Douglas C. Throckmorton, "Mixed Signals: The Administration's Policy on Marijuana—Part Four—the Health Effects and Science," US Food and Drug Administration, June 20, 2014. www.fda.gov.
9. Quoted in Christopher Ingraham, "After Legalization, Colorado Pot Arrests Plunge," *Washington Post*, March 26, 2015. www.washingtonpost.com.
10. Justice Louis Brandeis, dissenting, *New State Ice Co. v. Liebmann*, 1932.
11. International Narcotics Control Board, *Report of the International Narcotics Control Board for 2013*, p. 96.

12. Quoted in Madeleine Winer, "Some Warn Marijuana Legalization Could Bring More Addiction," *Arizona Republic* (Phoenix, AZ), August 21, 2015. www.azcentral.com.

13. Mohini Ranganathan and Deepak Cyril D'Souza, "The Acute Effects of Cannabinoids on Memory in Humans: A Review," *Psychopharmacology*, November 2006, p. 425. www.ncbi.nlm.nih.gov.

14. Andrew Zalesky et al., "Effect of Long-Term Cannabis Use on Axonal Fibre Connectivity," *Brain*, June 4, 2012. http://brain.oxfordjournals.org.

15. Quoted in News.com.au, "Marijuana Causes Brain Damage, Find Australian Scientists," August 9, 2012. www.news.com.au.

16. Quoted in Sullivan Moore, "This Is Your Brain on Drugs."

17. Marta Di Forti et al., "Proportion of Patients in South London with First-Episode Psychosis Attributable to Use of High Potency Cannabis: A Case-Control Study," *Lancet*, March 2015. www.thelancet.com.

18. Louisa Degenhardt et al., "The Persistence of the Association Between Adolescent Cannabis Use and Common Mental Disorders into Young Adulthood," *Addiction*, January 2013, p. 124. www.ncbi.nlm.nih.gov.

19. Meier et al., "Persistent Cannabis Users Show Neuropsychological Decline from Childhood to Midlife."

20. Marta Di Forti et al., "Confirmation That the AKT1 (rs2494732) Genotype Influences the Risk of Psychosis in Cannabis Users," *Biological Psychiatry*, November 15, 2012. www.ncbi.nlm.nih.gov.

21. Avshalom Caspi et al., "Moderation of the Effect of Adolescent-Onset Cannabis Use on Adult Psychosis by a Functional Polymorphism in the Catechol-O-Methyltransferase Gene: Longitudinal Evidence of a Gene X Environment Interaction," *Biological Psychiatry*, May 15, 2005, p. 1117. www.biologicalpsychiatryjournal.com.

22. Silvia Minozzi et al., "An Overview of Systematic Reviews on Cannabis and Psychosis: Discussing Apparently Con-

flicting Results," *Drug and Alcohol Review*, 2010. www.ncbi
.nlm.nih.gov.

23. Monique Jeanette Delforterie et al., "The Relationship Between Cannabis Involvement and Suicidal Thoughts and Be-
haviors," *Drug and Alcohol Dependence,* May 1, 2015, p. 98.
www.ncbi.nlm.nih.gov.

24. Edmund Silins et al., "Young Adult Sequelae of Adolescent
Cannabis Use: An Integrative Analysis," *Lancet Psychiatry*,
September 2014, p. 286. www.thelancet.com.

25. Michael T. Lynskey et al., "Major Depressive Disorder, Suicidal
Ideation, and Suicide Attempt in Twins Discordant for Cannabis Dependence and Early-Onset Cannabis Use," *JAMA Psychiatry,* October 2004. http://archpsyc.jamanetwork.com.

26. Murray A. Mittleman et al., "Triggering Myocardial Infarction
by Marijuana, *Circulation*, June 12, 2001. www.ncbi.nlm.nih
.gov.

27. Emilie Jouanjus et al., "Cannabis Use: Signal of Increasing
Risk of Serious Cardiovascular Disorders," *Journal of the
American Heart Association*, April 23, 2014. http://jaha.aha
journals.org.

28. Peter Gates et al., "Cannabis Smoking and Respiratory
Health: Consideration of the Literature," *Respirology*, July
2014, p. 655.

29. Gates et al., "Cannabis Smoking and Respiratory Health:
Consideration of the Literature," p. 657.

30. American Medical Association, "H-95.998 AMA Policy Statement on Cannabis," November 2013. www.ama-assn.org.

31. Tauheed Zaman et al., *Position Statement on Marijuana as
Medicine,* American Psychiatric Association, 2013, p. 1.
www.psychiatry.org.

Chapter 3: Is Marijuana an Effective Medical Treatment?

32. US Food and Drug Administration Dockets, "Marinol," 2004.
www.fda.gov.

33. Jörg Wissel et al., "Low Dose Treatment with the Synthetic Cannabinoid Nabilone Significantly Reduces Spasticity-
Related Pain: A Double-Blind Placebo-Controlled Cross-Over

Trial," *Journal of Neurology*, September 20, 2006. www.ncbi
.nlm.nih.gov.

34. US Food and Drug Administration, "Fast Track, Breakthrough
Therapy, Accelerated Approval, Priority Review," September
14, 2015. www.fda.gov.

35. American Epilepsy Society, "AES Position on Medical Marijuana," March 21, 2016. www.aesnet.org.

36. Throckmorton, "Mixed Signals: The Administration's Policy on
Marijuana—Part Four—the Health Effects and Science."

37. Raymond J.M. Niesink and Margriet W. van Laar, "Does Cannabidiol Protect Against Adverse Psychological Effects of
THC?," *Frontiers in Psychiatry*, October 16, 2013. www.ncbi
.nlm.nih.gov.

38. Traute Demirakca et al., "Diminished Gray Matter in the Hippocampus of Cannabis Users: Possible Protective Effects of
Cannabidiol," *Drug and Alcohol Dependence*, April 1, 2011.
www.ncbi.nlm.nih.gov.

39. Niesink and Van Laar, "Does Cannabidiol Protect Against Adverse Psychological Effects of THC?"

40. F.M. Leweke et al., "Cannabidiol Enhances Anandamide Signaling and Alleviates Psychotic Symptoms of Schizophrenia,"
Translational Psychiatry, March 20, 2012. www.ncbi.nlm.nih
.gov.

41. US Food and Drug Administration, "FDA and Marijuana," February 9, 2016. www.fda.gov.

42. Quoted in Paula Reid and Stephanie Condon, "DEA Chief
Says Medical Marijuana 'Is a Joke,'" CBS News, November 4,
2015. www.cbsnews.com.

43. Suzanne Ryan-Ibarra et al., "Prevalence of Medical Marijuana
Use in California, 2012," *Drug and Alcohol Review*, September 26, 2014. www.ncbi.nlm.nih.gov.

44. Penny Berg Neadeau, interview with the author, May 8, 2016.

45. Quoted in Peter Hecht, "California Police Have No Interest
in Setting Pot Rules," *Sacramento Bee*, January 26, 2014.
www.sacbee.com.

46. Quoted in California NORML, "Medical Marijuana Patient
Population in CA," 2014. http://canorml.org.

47. Bertha K. Madras, interview with the author, May 7, 2016.

48. Throckmorton, "Mixed Signals: The Administration's Policy on Marijuana—Part Four—the Health Effects and Science."

49. Paul Armentano, "Marijuana Is Not Addictive," in *Marijuana*, ed. Arthur Gillard. Detroit: Greenhaven Press, 2009. At Issue. Rpt. from "Setting the Record Straight on Marijuana and Addiction," LewRockwell.com, 2008. *Opposing Viewpoints in Context*. Web. 8 May 2016.

50. National Institutes of Health, *NIDA Research Report Series: Marijuana*, p. 4.

51. American Psychiatric Association, *Diagnostic and Statistical Manual of Mental Disorders,* 5th ed. Arlington, VA: American Psychiatric Publishing, 2013, p. 325.

52. American Psychiatric Association, *Diagnostic and Statistical Manual of Mental Disorders,* p. 326.

53. American Psychiatric Association, *Diagnostic and Statistical Manual of Mental Disorders,* p. 326.

54. American Psychiatric Association, *Diagnostic and Statistical Manual of Mental Disorders,* p. 329.

55. Armentano, "Marijuana Is Not Addictive."

56. Deborah S. Hasin et al., "Prevalence of Marijuana Use Disorders in the United States Between 2001–2002 and 2012–2013," *JAMA Psychiatry*, December 2015. www.ncbi.nlm.nih.gov.

57. United Nations Office on Drugs and Crime, *Cannabis: A Short Review*. New York: United Nations, 2011, p. 6.

58. Ken C. Winters and Chih-Yuan S. Lee, "Likelihood of Developing an Alcohol and Cannabis Use Disorder During Youth: Association with Recent Use and Age," *Drug and Alcohol Dependency,* January 1, 2008. www.ncbi.nlm.nih.gov.

59. R.C. Callaghan et al., "All-Cause Mortality Among Individuals with Disorders Related to the Use of Methamphetamine: A Comparative Cohort Study," *Drug and Alcohol Dependency*, October 1, 2012. www.ncbi.nlm.nih.gov.

60. Susan Shapiro, "So You Think Marijuana Isn't Addictive," *Chicago Tribune*, January 7, 2015. www.chicagotribune.com.

61. Denise B. Kandel, "Stages in Adolescent Involvement in Drug Use," *Science*, November 28, 1975. http://science.sciencemag.org.

62. Roberto Secades-Villa et al., "Probability and Predictors of the Cannabis Gateway Effect: A National Study," *International Journal on Drug Policy*, February 2015. www.ncbi.nlm.nih.gov.

63. Andrea Weinberger et al., "Is Cannabis Use Associated with an Increased Risk of Onset and Persistence of Alcohol Use Disorders? A Three-Year Prospective Study Among Adults in the United States," *Drug and Alcohol Dependency,* April 1, 2016. www.ncbi.nlm.nih.gov.

64. Marco Pistis et al., "Adolescent Exposure to Cannabinoids Induces Long-Lasting Changes in the Response to Drugs of Abuse of Rat Midbrain Dopamine Neurons," *Biological Psychiatry*, July 15, 2004.

65. National Institutes of Health, *NIDA Research Report Series: Marijuana*, p. 7.

66. NORML, "FAQs: Critics Claim That Marijuana Is a 'Gateway Drug.' How Do You Respond to This Charge?" http://norml.org.

67. Secades-Villa et al., "Probability and Predictors of the Cannabis Gateway Effect: A National Study."

68. Quoted in Ron Snyder, "Experts Debate Whether Marijuana Is a 'Gateway' Drug," ABC 2 News, February 16, 2014. www.abc2news.com.

Chapter 5: Should Marijuana Be Decriminalized?

69. Quoted in Ian Lovett, "In California, Marijuana Is Smelling More like Big Business," *New York Times*, April 11, 2016. www.nytimes.com.

70. Quoted in WSPA News, "How Is Colorado Doing Since Marijuana Legalization?," October 30, 2015. http://wspa.com.

71. Quoted in WSPA News, "How Is Colorado Doing Since Marijuana Legalization?"

72. Quoted in Scott Keyes, "Colorado's Marijuana Tax Revenues Nearly Double Last Year's Figures," *Guardian* (Manchester), September 21, 2015. www.theguardian.com.

73. Christopher Ingraham, "After Legalization, Colorado Pot Arrests Plunge," *Washington Post*, March 26, 2015. www.washingtonpost.com.

74. Federal Bureau of Investigation, "2014 Crime in the United States," 2015. www.fbi.gov.

75. Quoted in Chris Isidore, "Fatal Accidents Involving Stoned Drivers Soared in Washington Since Pot Was Legalized," CNNMoney, May 10, 2016. www.money.cnn.com.

76. Kevin Wong and Chelsey Clarke, *The Legalization of Marijuana in Colorado: The Impact*, vol 3. Denver: Rocky Mountain High Intensity Drug Trafficking Area, 2015. www.rmhidta.org.

77. Wong and Clarke, *The Legalization of Marijuana in Colorado: The Impact*.

78. United Nations Office on Drugs and Crime, *World Drug Report 2014*, p. 44.

79. Lloyd D. Johnston et al., *Monitoring the Future: National Survey Results on Drug Use 1975–2015: 2015 Overview: Key Findings on Adolescent Drug Use*. Ann Arbor: Institute for Social Research, University of Michigan, 2016, p. 5.

80. Quoted in Steven Nelson, "Pot Use Among Colorado Teens Appears to Drop After Legalization," *U.S. News & World Report*, August 7, 2014. www.usnews.com.

81. *The Legalization of Marijuana in Colorado: The Impact: Latest Results for Colorado Youth and Adult Marijuana Use*. Denver: Rocky Mountain High Intensity Drug Trafficking Area, 2016, p. 2.

82. *The Legalization of Marijuana in Colorado: The Impact*, p. 2.

Americans for Safe Access (ASA)

National Office
1806 Vernon St. NW, Suite 300
Washington, DC 20009
phone: (202) 857-4272
website: www.safeaccessnow.org

The ASA's mission is to ensure safe and legal access to marijuana for medical use and research. It advocates for patients' rights to have access to medical marijuana without persecution under the law.

Citizens Against Legalizing Marijuana (CALM)

PO Box 2995
Carmichael, CA 95608
phone: (916) 965-4825
website: www.calmusa.org

CALM is a volunteer political action committee dedicated to defeating any effort to legalize marijuana. It provides information about different topics regarding marijuana, as well as how people can get involved and take a stand against marijuana legalization.

Drug Policy Alliance (DPA)

925 Fifteenth St. NW, 2nd Floor
Washington, DC 20005
phone: (202) 683-2030
website: www.drugpolicy.org

Actively involved in the legislative process, the DPA is the nation's leading organization promoting drug policies based on compassion and human rights. It works to reverse laws it considers harmful to society and works to promote policy reform.

Marijuana Policy Project (MPP)

PO Box 77492
Capitol Hill

Washington, DC 20013
phone: (202) 462-5747
website: www.mpp.org

Founded in January 1995, the MPP is the largest organization in the United States focused on ending marijuana prohibition. It is working to change federal law prohibiting recreational use of the drug and to allow states to determine their own marijuana policies and regulation free of federal interference.

National Institute on Drug Abuse (NIDA)

Office of Science Policy and Communications
Public Information and Liaison Branch
6001 Executive Blvd.
Room 5213, MSC 9561
Bethesda, MD 20892
phone: (301) 443-1124
website: www.drugabuse.gov

The NIDA is a US federal government research institution whose mission is to use science to examine the issues of drug abuse and addiction. The organization offers information on the latest science, trends, and statistics regarding drug abuse.

National Organization for the Reform of Marijuana Laws (NORML)

1100 H St. NW, Suite 830
Washington, DC 20005
phone: (202) 483-5500
website: www.norml.org

NORML is working toward the legalization of responsible marijuana use by adults. It acts as an advocate for consumers to ensure access to high-quality marijuana that is safe and affordable. Its website includes information regarding marijuana laws, research, and more.

Partnership for Drug-Free Kids

352 Park Ave. S., 9th Floor
New York, NY 10010
phone: 212-922-1560
website: www.drugfree.org

Previously known as Partnership for a Drug Free America, Partnership for Drug-Free Kids is a nonprofit organization dedicated to reducing teen drug abuse and helping families affected by drug abuse. Its website offers the most current information regarding drug abuse as well as support for those affected by it.

Students for Sensible Drug Policy (SSDP)

1011 O St. NW #1
Washington, DC 20001
phone: (202) 393-5280
website: www.ssdp.org

The SSDP is an international network of students concerned about the impact of drug abuse on their communities. Its goal is to empower young people to participate in the political process and push for sensible policies for a safer future and to fight back against counterproductive policies that directly harm youth.

US Food and Drug Administration (FDA)

10903 New Hampshire Ave.
Silver Spring, MD 20993
phone: (888) 463-6332
website: www.fda.gov

The FDA is the federal government agency responsible for the regulation and safety of the nation's food and drug supply, including marijuana-based medications. It oversees the scientific approval of innovations that improve medicine, making it safer and more effective for the public and for providing the public with cohesive information about medications.

Books

Jonathan Caulkins, Angela Hawkin, Beau Kilman, and Mark Kleiman, *Marijuana Legalization: What Everyone Needs to Know*. New York: Oxford University Press, 2012.

Martin A. Lee, *Smoke Signals: A Social History of Marijuana— Medical, Recreational, and Scientific*. New York: Scribner, 2013.

Roger Roffman, *Marijuana Nation: One Man's Chronicle of America Getting High: From Vietnam to Legalization*. New York: Pegasus, 2014.

Mark Haskell Smith, *Heart of Dankness: Underground Botanists, Outlaw Farmers, and the Race for the Cannabis Cup*. New York: Broadway, 2012.

Jon Walker, *After Legalization: Understanding the Future of Marijuana Policy*. Washington, DC: FDL Writers Foundation, 2014.

Internet Sources

CNN Transcripts, "Weed: A Dr. Sanjay Gupta Investigation," August 11, 2013. http://transcripts.cnn.com/TRANSCRIPTS/1308/11/se.01.html.

David Kelly, "Pot Sales Healing Economic Woes of the Colorado Town of DeBeque," *Los Angeles Times,* April 4, 2016. www.latimes.com/nation/la-na-cannabis-city-colorado-20160404-story.html.

Joshua Miller, "In Colorado, A Look at Life After Marijuana Legalization," *Boston Globe*, February 22, 2016. www.bostonglobe.com/metro/2016/02/21/from-colorado-glimpse-life-after-marijuana-legalization/rcccuzhMDWV74UC4IxXIYJ/story.html.

Susan Shapiro, "So You Think Marijuana Isn't Addictive," *Chicago Tribune*, January 7, 2015. www.chicagotribune.com/news/opinion/commentary/ct-addict-marijuana-legalize-dylan-cheech-chong-perspec-0108-jm-20150107-story.html.

Hampton Sides, "Science Seeks to Unlock Marijuana's Secrets," *National Geographic*, June 2015. http://ngm.nationalgeographic.com/2015/06/marijuana/sides-text.

Steve Sternberg, "Marijuana as Medicine," *U.S. News & World Report*, October 13, 2015. http://health.usnews.com/health-news/patient-advice/articles/2015/10/13/marijuana-as-medicine.

Joel Warner, "Marijuana Legalization: Could 2016 Be the Year Federal Law Derails the Cannabis Movement?," *International Business Times*, January 12, 2016. www.ibtimes.com/marijuana-legalization-could-2016-be-year-federal-law-derails-cannabis-movement-2258515.

Websites

Colorado Marijuana (www.colorado.gov/marijuana). The state of Colorado's website about marijuana includes news, public health advisories, and information about immediate and long-term health effects, addiction, marijuana law, and business.

PubMed (www.ncbi.nlm.nih.gov/pubmed). Created by the National Center for Biotechnology Information, a federal agency, PubMed provides easily searchable access to 26 million abstracts for biomedical literature from life science journals and online books. The abstracts typically summarize the objectives, methods, results, and conclusions of each study. A list of related publications is displayed on each page.

World Health Organization (www.who.int/substance_abuse/facts/cannabis/en). The World Health Organization, an agency of the United Nations concerned with international public health, provides a global perspective on marijuana and other drugs. The site contains links to illicit substance terminology, classification, facts and figures, activities, publications, and research tools.

PICTURE CREDITS

Cover: iStockphoto.com/David Strange

6: Depositphotos/littleny

9: Depositphotos/EpicStockMedia

13: Depositphotos/photographee.eu

17: Theo Stroomer/Getty Images

21: Staff/MCT/Newscom

26: Depositphotos/toxawww

29: Associated Press

33: Associated Press/dpa

38: Living Art Enterprises/Science Photo Library

40: Associated Press

45: Depositphotos/GeniusKp

49: John Moore/Getty Images

50: Depositphotos/Wavebreakmedia

54: Luiz Rampelotta/Sipa USA/Newscom

59: Associated Press

62: Joe Raedle/Getty Images